THIS IS VOLUME II

IN

The Pioneer Heritage Series

D1316897

WESTERN STORY

THE RECOLLECTIONS

OF CHARLEY O'KIEFFE

1884-1898

With an introduction by

A . B . GUTHRIE , JR .

UNIVERSITY OF NEBRASKA PRESS • 1960

*These recollections
are most reverently dedicated
to the most wondrous faculty of Memory,
God's greatest gift to man.*

INTRODUCTION

BECAUSE MEMORY so often is faulty, reminiscences are suspect. The researcher and even the casual student prefer diaries, for recorded in them, as of the dates of entry, are the then-and-there experiences still fresh in mind.

It seems advisable to open an introduction to WESTERN STORY with this simple truth because here, by all appearances, is the exception. Though elderly, Author Charley O'Kieffe is very much at himself. Evidence and impression indicate a memory extraordinarily clear and exact. Where it fails him, he says so—when he does not resolve his uncertainties by reference to accepted records.

Though not too familiar with the section he writes about, or its history, I speak with a sizeable assurance, and not only for the one reason I shall name.

In point of time I came along somewhat later than O'Kieffe. In point of experience I am almost his contemporary, for as settlers kept pushing into the American plains the beginning ways of life in eastward regions were repeated in those westward. His Nebraska, thus, was much like the Montana of my boyhood. Nowhere was the duplication exact, to be sure. Geography, climate and many other factors made some difference. Yet a great similarity remained.

So I can confirm—and with the warmth of rediscovery—item after item of O'Kieffe's account. He jars out of memory the circumstances of my early life. Here is how I lived. Here are the rude techniques of those times, here the simple pleasures, the chores and projects, the green embarrassments, the hard aspirations, the little, important things of field and household.

It was in 1884 that the O'Kieffes went by wagon to the Sandhills of Nebraska. The author was a small boy then, a small boy in a numerous family which a long-suffering and resolute mother led. (The father hardly enters this chronicle; he had disappeared into the mists somewhere.) In northwestern Nebraska, in the vicinities of Gordon and Rushville, Charley O'Kieffe grew to adolescence; and it is mostly about those years that he writes.

No cowpuncher story, this. No reflection of the great western myth. It could be called a homesteader chronicle, though not with entire justice. It is a story of people adjusting themselves to a strange and hard environment, of communities struggling into being. The author describes it best:

> On the pages that follow, you will find little of romance, no heroes either real or made up, no hired gunslingers, no hell-raisin' but safe cowpunchers. You will find much of love, mostly of the silent sort, hope coupled with hard work, some suffering, lots of privation, a little real heroism, and a few incidents of downright meanness.

Call it, finally, the story of young Charley O'Kieffe, told by a man of kindliness and gentle humor who expresses himself, if not with brilliance, then with welcome clarity.

Introduction

It is hardly enough to say that residents and ex-residents of Nebraska and particularly of Sheridan County should welcome this volume. It will please other readers and endure as a source.

And it is, incidentally, an example of the best service of a university press.

A. B. GUTHRIE, JR.

CONTENTS

*A map of Sheridan County and Pine Ridge
Reservation appears on page 109*

[xi]

TO THE READER

Today I am seventy-seven, and while I can still think clearly and remember distinctly it seems proper that I should start writing down a few incidents and describe a few people that were a part of my life from 1884, when our family joined others in the trek from Back East to Out West, to 1898 when I left Northwestern Nebraska. This will not be a historical record or an autobiography, but a little bit of each.

So far as I know, no expert has fixed the point where memory begins to work, but in my own case the ability to recall goes back to somewhere in my fourth year. This means that anything I tell about which happened before that time was described to me by someone older who had witnessed the event.

On the pages that follow, you will find little of romance, no heroes either real or made up, no hired gun-slingers, no hell-raisin' but safe cowpunchers. You will find much of love, mostly of the silent sort, hope coupled with hard work, some suffering, lots of privation, a little real heroism, and a few incidents of downright meanness.

During our first years in Northwestern Nebraska we had no books, no magazines, no newspapers. The first paper that came into our home was called *The Hearthstone*, a four-sheeter filled with a hodgepodge of reading matter and get-rich-quick, get-well-safely advertising. When it had been read by all of us who knew how, this publication was destined to become shelf covering or was reserved for singeing chickens or maybe eventually some of it found its way to the little gray hut out behind the house, but there we depended mostly on corncobs. The lack of things to read or talk about led us youngsters to the habit of listening to what others had to say when they dropped by on their way to town or—if from a distance—to stay all night with us. Quite often these chance visitors had some pretty interesting tales to tell, and we small ones listened eagerly. Our house was not so big that we could not hear from every nook and corner, especially from behind the stove. That many, if not all, of these tales had little or no foundation in fact was of no concern to us. If later on they should prove to be entirely untrue, even slanderous, who cared? Those who spread the tales had no property that might be seized in case of suit for defamation of character, while even the best of men in that section might not relish having his past probed too deeply or his present conduct screened too closely. But yarns are one thing and the truth another, which is why I do not include here any tales of treacherous, quick-on-the-draw bad men or heroic, quicker-on-the-draw peace officers. I did not see or meet any, so why lie about it?

Among the scores of cowpunchers that I knew personally between 1884 and 1898, none were crack shots although they all could shoot straight enough when the need arose, such as for the purpose of chasing off some sneaky coyote or ending the sufferings of a horse who had broken his leg and could not be saved. (And of course a rattlesnake was always an inviting target as such reptiles had no friends among man or beast.) Most of these boys were good horsemen, handy with the rope for legitimate uses, and all capable of doing the daily tasks on the average ranch. None were even fair singers, most of them not even able to carry a tune, while if any of them had dared to bring such a thing as a guitar into the bunkhouse he'd have been reminded that the ranch was a place for hard work, and when the day's tasks were done what was wanted was sweet slumber, not sweet music. In other words, I've seen many more of the Gabby Hayes type of ranch hand than the Roy Rogers breed. I do not say they never actually existed, but I do affirm they were not as common as cactus.

In my opinion a great disservice has been done to the West—or that part of the country which I knew as the West—by the far too many tales of romance, fierce gunplay, and clever escape from the enemy. The type of men who gave rise to fiction characters were vastly outnumbered by the real sterling and steady men and women whose lives were spent doing the work as it needed to be done, with none of the thrills and frills that form the basis of Hollywood and television portrayals of early Western life.

To me, the best features of Mari Sandoz' *Old Jules* are the things most missing in other Western tales. In her book Mari introduces real persons who did their work as best they could without fuss or feathers, even though now and then one of them had to do a little dirty job on some person or community as part of the process of developing the country. Her book is not filled with villains or heroes. Her characters are mostly just plain people behaving as conditions seemed to warrant—at times low, at times rising to heights, but always human and natural.

If in my book I leave the impression that nothing but drab incidents of daily life appeal to me, please charge it to the harsh and somewhat bitter years of my growing up.

The reason for so many dark pictures is that there is no way I can gloss over or eliminate the eternal hard problems of fuel and food, clothing and equipment. They were facts of life that had to be faced every day. But we had so little back where we came from, and that little promised to become less had we stayed there, so, as you will see, we actually moved from pretty bad to—not so worse.

Sincerely,

Charley O'Kieffe

CHARLES D. O'KIEFFE

July 5, 1956
Minneapolis, Minnesota

WESTERN STORY

I

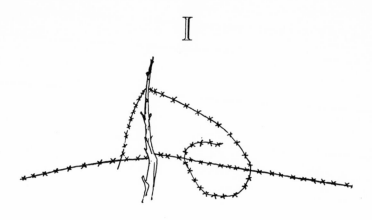

WE GO WEST

*Who I am and something about the O'Kieffe family;
and why we went West*

As a lad I was nearly always called "Mrs. O'Kieffe's little boy Charley." In my adult years—during which I traveled in forty-five states and worked at a total of forty-six different jobs—I became Mr. O'Kieffe. Today at seventy-seven I am called Grandpa by ten grandchildren, although the youngest, little Susan, says it is Grandpa Charley.

Naturally, the first event in my life was being born, which occurred on July 5, 1879. According to what I've been told, Mother herded cattle all day long in the broiling hot sun so the children could attend a Fourth of July celebration in a nearby community. The next morning around two A.M. I was born. No doctor, no nurse, no midwife, just

Mother and God; and two days later she was up and doing her regular housework.

There was no record made of my birth excepting an entry in our old family Bible, which, along with most all of our earthly goods, was destined to go up in smoke in the wreck of a westbound train. Not until a few years ago, while doing war work, was I able to collect enough data to satisfy the authorities in Lincoln, Nebraska, and obtain what they called a deferred birth certificate. This has proved completely legal, so now I know it is more than just hearsay—I was actually born.

The place of my birth was a rented farm some eight miles south of Tecumseh, Johnson County, Nebraska. While I was still small enough to be confined in a clothes-basket crib, we moved to another farm about ten miles north of Tecumseh; and it was from this spot that we began our western trip. But before we get started West, you should meet the other members of the family and know something of the origin of the O'Kieffe clan.

In the beginning, there was John, who arrived steerage from the Old Sod at somewhere around fourteen years of age. I've been told by those who knew him that he was a strapping big fellow who would rather fight than eat. Just how or where he spent the days of his early young manhood is not a matter of record. All we know is that shortly before the Civil War broke out he landed in Portage, Wisconsin, where he became a raftsman for a lumber company.

At about this time in eastern Pennsylvania a young girl was growing into womanhood. Her name was Mary Elizabeth Gayman, and she was the daughter of an industrious and thrifty Scotchman and his hard-working wife of Pennsylvania Dutch stock. How and when they met we never learned, but John O'Kieffe and Mary Gayman were married at Portage, on December 31, 1860. Because of the destruction of our Bible, in which such information was kept, we cannot be sure as to the age of the bride and groom. However, I frequently heard Mother tell people that she was born in 1841, which would have made her nineteen at the time of her marriage.

From this union came nine additional O'Kieffes, whom I now present in the order of their arrival:

> *Jack,* probably named John, no birth record
> *Helen Arabelle,* born December 13, 1863
> *Ulysses S. Grant,* born July 11, 1866
> *Abner Van Rensselear,* born December 28, 1868
> *Ira J.,* born April 11, 1870
> *Lula Mae,* died in infancy
> *Minnie Blanche,* born June 3, 1875
> *George Andrew,* born May 11, 1877
> *Charles DeWitt,* born July 4-5, 1879

In view of the fact that none of us were baptized, one name would have done just as well as another, but where some of them came from has always been a mystery to me. Surely no relatives on either side passed them along to my parents, and as both Father and Mother were entirely without schooling they could hardly have gotten them out of books. Excepting our family Bible, to my knowledge there was not a single piece of printed matter—book, magazine, or newspaper—in our home until I was around ten years old. (I did have a few dog-eared schoolbooks after I was six or seven.) No doubt Grant owed his three-name handle to the part his namesake had played in the recently ended Civil War, in which our father fought for thirty months. As for Abner, he never had knee breeches with silver buckles nor did he at any time or in any way display any of the aristocratic traits you might connect with the original Van Rensselear,* Dutch Governor of New York. And as for me,

---

* Who spelled it Van Rensselaer.—*Editor's note*

I never was let in on the reason for my middle name of De-Witt. Around the time I was born, the Reverend T. DeWitt Talmage was gaining quite a reputation as a powerful preacher, and there is the possibility that his name and fame made such an impression on my parents that they bestowed part of it on me. Well, regardless of their reason, I have no cause for complaint and have passed it along to a fine son and he in turn to his finer son.

Because this book is concerned with events and incidents in which I personally participated or was an eye-witness to, my father does not come into it from now on. I never saw him but twice in my whole life, and each time it was only for a few minutes. In 1885, after we had moved to Sheridan County, word came to us that he had passed away and was buried in the G.A.R. section of the cemetery in Tecumseh. From what Mother told me, he was not an ideal father and many times had caused her both heartbreak and hardship.

Mother was patient, long-suffering, and kind, although entirely undemonstrative when it came to showing affection. (Unless it might have happened when I was a very small baby, never a kiss from the opposite sex touched my lips until I went to Omaha in 1898.) In fairness to Mother, her lack of demonstrativeness was, I believe, the result of year after year of living under conditions that seemed to offer little, if any, hope for improvement. Her relentless uphill struggle for the very existence of herself and her children forced her to exhibit the practical to others and to conceal the sentimental. This was most in evidence when the boys grew up and one by one went away to start on their own. As I watched each in turn walk away from our old sod house, I saw no tears, no farewell kiss, not even a handshake. All that passed between them and Mother was that old commonplace, "Write when you get work." This attitude of Mother's may explain why she never told any of us younger children about our brother Jack, who had left home many years before I was born. In her matter-of-fact mind she had assumed that Jack was dead, and so never spoke of him.

Disappointed and discouraged almost continuously but never completely broken, Mother had dreams of a better life somewhere, some time. With my birth she became more determined than ever to end her old, very unhappy existence and start all over in a new country under what she hoped would be more favorable conditions and where at least she would have greater freedom.

During the summer of 1884, she and brother Grant drove out to Sheridan County, Nebraska, with a small team and light wagon. They both filed on homesteads about ten miles southeast of Rushville and some fourteen miles southwest of Gordon—two small villages just getting started in this new section of Nebraska.* Grant remained there to build a sod house, half on his claim and half on Mother's, which adjoined.

When Mother returned to our Johnson County home—just how, I never learned—the first question I asked her was, "Did the Indians scalp you, Maw?" They hadn't, but she almost scalped us. We had not been given too much attention during her absence, and had picked up a lot of head lice. But a vigorous scrubbing with coal oil killed off the pests, and in a few days we were back to normal in every way.

---

* Notes on the founding and organization of Sheridan County, Gordon, and Rushville begin on page 206.—*Editor's note*

*We leave Johnson County in our new covered wagon
with three milk cows tied to each side*

On September 15, 1884, about ten in the morning, our caravan moved out on a journey which was to require six weeks
and cover five hundred or more miles, including detours.
I could not help looking back several times as we started to
roll westward, and more than seventy years later I can still
see the row of tall trees that bordered the road leading away
from our old home, now deserted and desolate.

The O'Kieffes taking part in this exodus were Mother;
brother Ira, fourteen; sister Minnie, nine; brother George,
about seven; and myself, five—seen but not heard very
much. Of our worldly goods, the heavier and more bulky
stuff—implements, household effects, sewing machine, family records, Bible, and pictures—had been loaded into an
immigrant car to be shipped by freight to our destination.
The less cumbersome items and those we felt we could use
to advantage on our trip were stowed away in the bottom
of our wagon.

This was not a Conestoga, with its sway-back cover and
its snout-like projection at front and rear—which no doubt
is a familiar sight to you on movie and television screens.
(On this trip and several others, I never saw a Conestoga
wagon, but maybe they are considered to be more photo-
genic than what we used.) Our wagon was the ordinary
farm type, an Old Hickory as I recall. It was fairly new and
in good condition. In addition to the regular box or bed
that filled the space between the standards, we put on side
boards at the ends of both front and back bolsters. This
top-box, as it was called, gave us a total depth of close to
three feet. Multiply this by the length and width of the box
and you have quite a lot of storage space. Here was where
we packed our personal effects: at the bottom those less

likely to be needed, then items of current need, then the bedding—comforts, quilts, and nightgowns for Mother and Minnie. As was customary in those days, we boys slept in our underwear, homemade of red flannel for cold nights, though we preferred sleeping in the raw when it was warm enough.

Along the outside of the wagon box we had fastened hasps or clips properly spaced to receive the lower ends of the five ash bows that supported the canvas top of the outfit. The front bow was given a slight tilt forward so the driver would have some protection from rain or snow, yet still be able to see out on either side. At the rear, the canvas was fitted with a sort of puckering string by means of which the opening there could be almost completely closed and the whole run of canvas tightened when necessary. The cover was brand-new and the canvas shining white.

Hitched to the wagon and fitted with a new set of harness was our team of plow horses, gray Charley and bay Jim. Sometimes running loose, sometimes tied to the team was Prince, a handsome, clean-cut Hambletonian which we planned to use as a driving horse after we had made good and could afford a top-buggy.

Attached to the rear of the wagon by its long tongue was our masterpiece, a "caboose" consisting of the running gears of our cultivator with as big a chicken coop as it would take mounted securely between the wheels. (The beams and shovels of the cultivator had been dismantled and packed in the freight car with our heavy goods.) Twenty-four of our very finest Plymouth Rock hens and one rooster rode in the coop on its cultivator chassis. To their everlasting credit, in spite of the constant jerking and jostling week after week, these faithful old biddies kept us well supplied with good, full-shelled, rich eggs.

We tied our milk cows along the wagon, three to a side, with ropes of varying lengths so each could drift into a comfortable position as the caravan moved on. Nearly all cows were horned in those days as de-horning had not become a general practice and the hornless breed had not yet been developed. Consequently, each cow had plenty of anchorage for her individual rope around her personal horns, made fast just at the roots where the horn ended and the cow began. Being led mile after mile by their horns was a new experience for the girls, and in a day or two we had to remove the ropes and wrap the nooses with cotton batting and whatever soft leather we could find. Otherwise we wouldn't have been able to move them at all, and cows were vital to our life in the new country.

Mother sat on the front seat acting as pilot and at her side was Ira, doing the driving. Inside the wagon, but where she could see out and keep track of what was going on, was Minnie, while George and myself were "floaters"—sometimes inside the wagon, sometimes outside, but wherever we were taking everything in with pop eyes. As for the other members of the family, Grant was already in the West, Belle was married, and Ab was working on the farm of a Johnson County man rich enough to pay him $10.00 a month half the year and his board the other half.

When we started out there were two extra boys in our caravan—Charley and Fred Wasmund, sons of our neighbors. They had yoked together two young heifers and hooked them to a light spring wagon, their plan being to go out west, work for someone else, and let their heifers produce. Thus by the time the boys came of age and could take up land, they would have a good start of livestock. There was nothing wrong with the plan, but we hadn't gone two miles before the yoke broke and was found to be beyond repair. So Fred was sent back home with the heifers and Charley joined our entourage.

There was one more member of our party who can't possibly be left out: my pal Jack, a dog I'd grown up with—

in fact you might say that we were puppies together. Jack was a good dog, fairly large, but entirely unpedigreed. Folks told me later that he must have been at least half bull-dog, deducing this from his willingness as well as his ability to fight, and from his bowed legs. But they didn't know the secret of how he came by those legs, which is as follows. Partly to avoid the confusion behind and all around the wagon and partly because it was shady, Jack quickly adopted the rear axle as his traveling position and—with occasional excursions for personal reasons—stayed right under it during the trip. The space between the ground and the wagon axle being about four inches less than Jack's normal height, he was forced to crouch, and keeping this up day after day was to give him those beautifully bowed legs.

Mother and Ira kept pretty close to the job of piloting our tour, but George and myself and our stowaway, Charley Wasmund, swarmed all over the caravan, sometimes running ahead of the slow-moving outfit and then lagging behind when we came across something of extra interest. Every so often, of course, we had to check up on the cows —they were called Dutch and Fawny and Brindle, White Tail and Crumple Horn. The sixth one will just have to forgive me as I have clean forgotten her name.

We didn't travel very far the first day, making our first night's camp near Sterling, then a small village on the road from Tecumseh to Lincoln. This was long before the state got so settled up that "Keep Off" and "No Trespassing" signs had sprouted all over the outdoors. We just stopped where we could see both wood and water, and prepared to make ourselves comfortable. First we took out our sheet-iron camp stove and our few cooking utensils, then what food was on hand, and we were all set up for light housekeeping. If the weather was quiet and the surroundings right, we often built a campfire instead of using the stove, which was much more fun for us youngsters.

After that first evening meal out under the blue sky, we sat around for a bit and then turned in for the night. Mother and Minnie slept in the forepart of the wagon and George and I in the rear. Ira and Charley Wasmund bunked under an improvised tent made by raising the end of the wagon tongue to the full height of the neckyoke to serve as a ridgepole, and spreading a tarpaulin over it. Here they slept very comfortably and were always quickly available in an emergency. Apparently the hens and their rooster pal did not suffer any inconvenience; and as for old Jack, all he had to do was lie down right where he had been walking in order to enjoy his canine dreams.

On the way: some more or less upsetting incidents including my first encounter with the Iron Horse

Many another covered wagon ahead of ours had passed through Lincoln, the capital city of Nebraska, but I doubt if any of them attracted as much attention from the onlookers as did our outfit. The young rowdies along our route had many a smart remark to fling at us, but I, at least, was far too busy taking in the sights to pay much attention. This was my first view of so large a collection of buildings of so many different sizes and styles. It must have been a fairyland after dark when all the store windows were ablaze with light from the big lamps; but we did not tarry in Lincoln long enough for me to see what it was like at night when they were lit. (I have never learned why some folks said "coal oil" and others "kerosene" when they were both talking about the same thing.)

Approaching Lincoln from the east-southeast, we hit the main street leading to the center of town. In the early days of our nation it was common for towns to be built around a central square in which was placed something of interest, and Lincoln was featuring a salt-water fountain which bubbled up in the middle of the square, the water being caught in a rather ornate basin. The street on which we came in— if I remember right, it was paved with cedar blocks—detoured around this fountain. No sooner had the cows smelled the water than they decided they had to have some of it—right now! The result was a wagon full of anxious people careening along behind a six-cow-plus-two-horse hitch, expecting at any moment to be upset right there in front of everybody. But luck was with us and the bossies reached the edge of the fountain without upsetting anything but our dignity. However, when they rammed their muzzles into the sparkling water, they were in for a surprise—good as it looked and smelled, the taste was very briny and medicinal. A startled sip or two and they were all set to move on to some place where the water was plainer.

Crossing the Platte River at Columbus—about sixty miles northwest of Lincoln as the crow flies, but a four-day journey as the caravan crawled—was the next high spot punctuating our long trek. In the dry season then prevailing, the river had dwindled to four little ribbons of water separated by sand bars covered with bushes. Spanning it was a wooden bridge, the longest we had come across so far. The vibration of many wagons rumbling over it through the years had caused the planks of the flooring to work loose at each end, and the spikes holding down the planks had worked up as much as a half inch or more. They were the old-fashioned handmade spikes, square and tapering toward the points, with large heads shaped somewhat like an oversized coffee bean or a pregnant watermelon seed. Guided by the kind of intuition which is built in teen-age boys, brother Ira discovered that if he tapped a nailhead at an angle with a hammer, it would pop off and make a very fine bit of ammunition for his slingshot. He had a nice pocketful of iron pellets by the time our caravan had completed the crossing.

These were to come in unexpectedly handy quite a bit later when we were crossing Brown County and went through a little village called Johnstown. As we started to drive down the main street, a gang of scalawags came running out and tried to stampede our cows. They almost succeeded in upsetting the wagon before Ira scared them off. But we'd gone on only a little ways when they were back again with reinforcements and a lot of rotten tomatoes and other garbage. When they began throwing it at us, Ira dug out his slingshot, loaded it with an iron spike head, and let fly, hitting one of the gang on the lobe of his ear. The sight of the blood spurting out cooled off the others, and we went on our way with no more trouble. But it was lucky for all concerned that the spike head hit just where it did. An inch or two farther up or to either side and our westward movement might have halted right there.

This was the only outside interference we had experienced thus far in our journey, although I was later to learn that the favorite pastime of town kids was to jump on and beat up country kids when they dared come into town. This attitude did not change until the farmer grew a bit more prosperous and became an economic factor to be reckoned with. Then he was courted by the local people and much visiting took place between them.

After we left Columbus we had kept on heading northwest, and for a week or so were still traveling in a well-settled section of Nebraska with fair-looking farms and homes all around us. I still can see in my mind's eye some of the towns we passed through as we moved slowly on from the real black-soil country into the semisandy sections.

We must have bought some supplies along the way, but I have no recollection of anything which had to do with the financial side of our trip—whether we had any money or supply problems. We ate pretty well and there was so much to see that how we got the food didn't give me any concern.

About two weeks after crossing the Platte we hit the main line of the Fremont, Elkhorn & Missouri Valley Railway * at O'Neill, where the branch line of this system came in from Sioux City. It was during this phase of our trip that I saw my first train. Our journey so far had been through farm land away from the tracks, and we had camped at points where trains did not pass or, if they did, they must have gone by when I slept. But now I made their acquaintance in a way I wasn't likely to forget.

We had penetrated far enough into the semisand country so that the tracks every now and then ran through deep cuts with sloping sand at either side of the roadbed. George and I did a lot of walking along the tracks because it was so much easier going than the loose sand through which our caravan was making its weary way. Also, someone had told us there was a chance of finding money that passengers had accidentally let fall from the train. At our age we did not bother to figure out the probabilities (or improbabilities) of garnering such a "windowfall," and were so intent on our treasure hunt that neither of us heard the noise of the train. Fortunately, it was a rather slow-moving freight. The first we knew of it was when the engineer pulled the whistle cord, causing the engine to emit a bloodcurdling shriek as it rounded the curve not too far away.

In one flying leap George was out of there and on top of the bank, but I was not so quick or so agile. In my fran-

---

* The line with the big elkhorn on the cupola of the caboose. It later became a part of the North-Western system.—*Author's note*

tic rush to get away from this horrifying monster, my feet kept slipping out from under me and my progress up the slope was something like·that of the frog in the well who hopped up two feet each day and slipped back one foot each night. But the fireman helped me out in what he probably thought was a very comical manner. As the engine puffed by, he reached out as far as he could and swatted me right on the back of my neck with his cap. That was all the incentive I needed to finish the trip to the top in nothing flat.

We run out of water and then into it; and in between
I see my first real Indian

Now that we had joined the F. E. & M. V. right-of-way, the wooden ties and steel rails were to be our guide for most of the rest of our journey. As we moved on the sand grew deeper, looser, and more powdery. Our progress slowed to a crawl, and our livestock as well as the wagon began to need more attention every day. The dry, loose sand rolled up with each turn of the wagon wheels and soon was grinding away at the axles. Frequent cleaning and greasing were necessary to keep the thimbles from wearing badly enough to cause a break, which would have been calamitous out in that lonely country. But the older heads in the family had enough sense to exercise utmost precaution, and we made the entire trip without a vehicle breakdown.

As well as keeping us from going astray, the F. E. & M. V. right-of-way also provided us with our water supply. There had been enough rain to fill up the ditches alongside the track in the low places where the roadbed had been graded up to the proper level, and from these we got all the water we needed for both animals and the human members of our party.

Then one blazing hot day in early October we found ourselves in trouble. How it happened I don't recall exactly—it might be that we had gotten away from the railroad, or that in the country we were passing through there had been no need to grade up the roadbed, or perhaps there hadn't been enough rain to fill the ditches—but for whatever reason, we were about out of water and there was none in sight. We had a small reserve of drinking water in the wagon, but none for cooking, and not a drop for the horses and cows and old Jack trotting beneath the rear axle with his tongue dry and lolling out of his mouth.

All day we traveled hopefully on, but darkness came and still no water. After a night of great anxiety we started out early, still clinging to the hope that just around the next mound of sand we would find another of those rainmade ponds. Along about ten in the forenoon, Jack came out from his shady nook, sniffed the dry air, and took off in a lope toward the north of our trail. In a few minutes he was back dripping wet and tried to tell us to follow him, which we did and soon came to a good supply of water. Here we camped and let the animals rest while we cleaned up, took a fine swim, and got all refurbished to continue our journey. You may be sure that Jack was now a hero to our group, and from that day until the day of his death he never lacked for a single thing that a dog could need or desire.

A day or two after we passed through Valentine and Fort Niobrara—from which later, at the time of the Sioux Rebellion, we got some of our armed forces—I saw my first real Indian. What would happen when we met an Indian was a matter to which a five-year-old boy was bound to give considerable thought, but even so I hardly knew just what to expect or what he might decide to do with us. However, when it finally took place, the meeting proved to be more of an anticlimax than anything. Instead of springing out of ambush and coming at us hell-for-leather and whooping, he was stuck with his wagon on the way up a steep sand hill.

Much has been said about the Indian being a good horseman, a fearless hunter, and a straight shooter with the bow and arrow; but he sure was not a good teamster. There the old fellow sat on his wagon seat, and all he could think of to do was try to shoo the horses by shaking the lines, and plead with them in his Sioux tongue, which they apparently did not understand or appreciate. At any rate, they just stood there sort of listless.

Brother Ira could not talk to the Indian, nor he to Ira, but the need of the moment was plain. Ira jumped down and unhitched our team by pulling out the pin that held the doubletree to the wagon tongue; then he hooked a short stay-chain into the loop at the end of the Indian's wagon tongue, and fastened the chain to our doubletree with a clevis. After that, all that was left to do was say "Giddap" to Charley and Jim, and away they went with the Indian wagon.

In the best way he knew, the Indian tried to express his appreciation, and Ira tried to make it clear that he was entirely welcome; and we hitched up again and went on. So our first encounter with the red man turned out to be just a normal incident of travel, and did not delay our journey more than a few minutes. I suppose if this were a Western story in the television tradition instead of a mere recital of true events, there would be another scene later on where this Oglala Sioux found us in a tight spot and came to our rescue. But we went our way and he went his, and never the twain did meet again.

Now that we were well into the Sandhills, our speed was that of a real slow snail going no place in particular. Our wagon wheels sank down into the sand halfway to the hubs and Charley and Jim had all they could do to pull the wagon along. But we kept moving on, ever westward now, and each day brought us a little nearer to our new home. Our trail was still along the railroad, and we were gradually coming closer to new construction, which meant more and looser sand, although here and there the way was more level, which helped the horses a bit.

One day about noon we came to a lake or large pond which we saw we'd have to ford as there did not seem to be any safe way to drive around it. It looked harmless enough. We could see green grass under the water at the edge, and that told us the lake must have been the recent creation of a rainstorm—although we had not been through any storms in the last few days.

There were wagon tracks going into the lake, and we decided that if others had crossed, so could we. But those wagon tracks must have been older than they looked. The going was fine for a few hundred feet; then the bottom dropped out. Water began to come through the bottom of the wagon box, and had it not been for our heavy belongings therein, I am sure the box would have floated out from between the standards. But we kept going and in a few minutes had made it through the deepest part of the lake and finally landed on the opposite side. Net result: every one of our chickens drowned and our belongings completely soaked.

Just as soon as the wagon was on dry ground, Mother went to work on a salvage job. In less time than it takes to tell it, she had wrung the neck of every fowl and hung it by its feet from a bush or stake so that it would bleed a little. Then we got everything out of the wagon, and for several days stayed right there while we got dehydrated and things put in order again.

Meanwhile Mother dressed and fried the chickens, and packed them down in lard so they would keep until we wanted to eat them. To this day I never see fried chicken without recalling the time that for once, through no fault of our own, we had more chicken than we wanted.

The end of our journey through the Sandhills; and our arrival at our new homestead

When we resumed our trek we could see that we were almost caught up with the railroad construction, as the grades became fresher looking and there were evidences of quite recent human habitation. Still, day after day, there was that weary monotony of crawling up and down the hills of loose, white sand—often the horses had to pull almost as hard downhill as up.

Late one afternoon we met a bearded old pirate headed our way driving a six-mule team with a heavy load of wool he was freighting from the Black Hills section to Omaha. As usual, Mother was up on the front seat beside Ira, and the rest of us were in the wagon, for it was no fun to be running around in this sort of soil condition. As the old bushwhacker neared our wagon, Mother hailed him to a halt. After the exchange of a few words, mostly from Mother to him, she said: "When will we get out of these pesky sandhills?"

"Lady," he said, "you will know when you get there, 'cause the last one is sure a son of a bitch."

And it sure was. Two days later we came to that last hill

with its vulgar name,* and as our worn team tugged its way down the final hard pull, we came to what they said was the east fork of Antelope Creek. Crossing this in an easy and safe ford, we landed on hard sand soil well covered with luxuriant grass which you can bet our horses and cows greatly enjoyed, and not too long after drove into Gordon, a hamlet of frame buildings housing a population of about 300 souls.

The sun had set and twilight had arrived when we drove out of Gordon headed in a southwesterly direction, on the home stretch at last. It was a clear night with a fairly bright moon. Nothing is quite so ethereal as the Western Nebraska moonlight—there is no smoke of industry to dim it and, because of the high and dry climate, no atmospheric fog.

For the first two or three miles there was a pretty well-marked road, but that soon began to fade out as the traffic spread in different directions. Though Mother knew but little about the way we were to go, she did know where we wanted to get to, so we stopped to make inquiries when we came to a lighted farm house. This happened to be the home of one Chris Burki, who later on was to dig a well for us.

After greetings, Mother asked if he knew where her son Grant O'Kieffe lived. Never heard of him, said Mr. Burki. Recalling a landmark from her previous trip, Mother said that as far as her memory went, Grant lived some three

* While the author will not commit himself, the "vulgar name" may well have been Squaw's Tit. According to Mari Sandoz, there are a number of hills which have been given this name. Rudolph Umland, in "Nebraska Not in the Guidebook," writes: "Driving through the sandhills . . . and noticing the contour of the hills made me think of the missionary in Somerset Maugham's story *Rain* who had neurotic dreams about these 'mountains of Nebraska' because they resemble female breasts. Early cowboys were aware of this resemblance too and named one of the mounds near Chadron 'Squaw's Tit'" (*Roundup: A Nebraska Reader*, Lincoln: University of Nebraska Press, 1957, p. 415)

miles to the west and a bit south of the Lone Butte—a hill which stuck out from the level land all around, much like a huge cone with a flattened top.

"Oh," said Chris after thinking it over. "You must mean Little Keefe."

Since he was not a very tall or big man, Mother decided this could be Grant; and Chris told us to keep on in the same direction we were headed and we would find our place. We thanked him; and then as we were driving away he called after us, "Did you folks get the news?"

We had no idea what news he meant, but one thing was sure—we hadn't been in any position to get any news from anybody about anything during our entire trip. Naturally, Mother asked Chris what he meant. "The railroad car where you had your goods went through a burning trestle between Wisner and Blair," he said. "Everything was burned up." And then, as an afterthought, "You folks are sure in a helluva fix, ain't you?"

We reached our new home sometime around midnight. (Pure guesswork: none of us had a watch and Grant had no clock.) Quarters were very cramped, but Grant made us all as comfortable as possible and soon we younger ones were fast asleep. As for my mother, I don't know what her thoughts were, this first night on the homestead which was to be our abiding place for some twelve years. She never showed any outward signs of her feelings about her loss; but she must have been deeply moved inside. Along with all the household effects on which we depended so much, there were lost Father's army-discharge papers and his old blue uniform, Mother's sewing machine, bolts of gingham, calico, cotton flannel, red flannel for underwear, denim for trousers, and all sorts of vegetable and flower seeds to help us get started raising food and to create a little bit of beauty around our new home.

As a matter of record, I might add that it took more than two years for Mother to reach a settlement with the railroad company. She got only $225.00 for everything, including her most prized and indispensable possession, her sewing machine. The railroad men said it was worth only $5.00, although for her it was as good as any new one, and would cost almost $100.00 to replace.

Where or when she got the inspiration I was never told, but Mother went to Rushville and borrowed the money to replace the things she so sorely needed from the bankers, Joe Thomas and Johnnie Jones, to whom she paid two per cent a month for seven years.

II

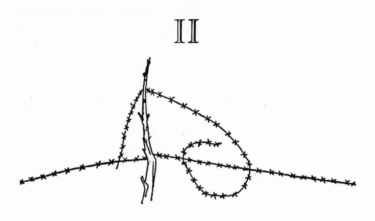

THE NEW LAND

*We get through our first winter thanks to faith,
hope, and buffalo chips*

WHEN WE AWOKE on November 5, 1884, our first
morning in our new home, we learned that a prairie
fire had recently passed over the land and everything was
bleak and bare. Now a prairie fire is an awesome thing to
behold and much worse to be a victim of, but in our neighborhood there was very little to sustain the blaze. Nothing
had been burned except the curly buffalo grass and other
dried-out bits of vegetation, and this left exposed just what
we needed—buffalo chips, the fuel of the prairie. Although
practically all those fine big animals had been killed off or
driven away before we got there, much to our joy and
comfort they had left behind their calling cards.

Here is the way the buffalo had unwittingly made fuel
to feed our home fires through our early years of pioneer-

ing. To start with, he ate his fill of the short but very nourishing grass that bears his name. Then this food went through the regular bovine digestive process and the residue was discharged as a semi-paste made up of the minerals and solids the buffalo did not want. Because of the high altitude and dry air of the western plains, this waste material formed into a sort of patty which, when completely dried out, became a straw-colored cake looking somewhat like a matzos or a small circle of Swedish health bread.

When we started out to gather our first chip harvest, the weather was bright but brisk for an early November day, so we wore all the warm clothing we owned, including such shoes as we possessed. Fortunately there was little cactus hazard since the fire had burned off the worst of their stinging spines, and we had nothing to fear from rattlesnakes as we did not live in or near their zone. These reptiles, who often rattled too late for their victims to save themselves, were found in that odd section of semihard sand lying across the Niobrara River, three miles to the south. In our neighborhood we had only the huge but harmless bull snake, the blue racer, and of course the ever-present garter snake.

We younger children had to cover as much ground as possible, gathering up all the chips we could find and putting them in piles. The older boys then loaded them on the wagon and hauled them home. There was virtually no odor left in the chips by the time we got our supply back to the house. They were water-repellent and could be piled up in the open without risk of serious deterioration, but we played safe and stacked our reserve supply in a sort of shed made of slabs Grant had gotten off the pine trees to the north of our place. In the kitchen, the chips were piled into the woodbox—an indispensable item found in every farm home, no matter where the folks might be living or what they used for fuel.

The chips were handled much as though they were chunks of box-board that had gotten wet and then been dried out. Soft coal, which many used later, was much messier and harder to handle; but once a coal fire was under way it burned longer and made less ash to blow around when a heavy gale sent the draft of the stove down instead of up.

For the edification of housewives who may never have cooked with buffalo chips, here is a rundown of the operations that Mother went through when making baking powder biscuits, for instance. It goes like this: Stoke the stove, get out the flour sack, stoke the stove, wash your hands, mix the biscuit dough, stoke the stove, wash your hands, cut out the biscuits with the top of a baking-powder can, stoke the stove, wash your hands, put the pan of biscuits in the oven, keep on stoking the stove until the biscuits are done. Mother had to go through this tedious routine three times a day excepting when what she was cooking did not require the use of the oven.

After about a year the original crop of buffalo chips had all been gathered and burned, so we had to start collecting what the cows had to contribute. Keeping about a month behind their droppings, we found enough cow chips dry enough for handling and burning to supplement our fuel supply. Eventually we had corncobs off our own land, and were given permission to cut pine trees off "No Man's Land," some forty miles north.

One day the exciting news came that a man in Gordon was paying $9.00 a ton for bones—any kind of bones: buffalo, steer, wolf, even human bones. After that, when we roamed the prairies picking up buffalo chips we gathered dry bones along with them. When enough had been accumulated to justify the fourteen-mile trip, off went the family wagon with its pay load. Thus our prairie land not only provided us fuel, but also a "bone-anza" to exchange for much-needed cash to buy food.

Thanks to a real mild winter we came through our first months on our homestead with no sickness and little real hunger. When spring came, all the older members of our family were in good shape both to start general farm work and to build the new sod house, which was to be the first real home Mother had known since her early girlhood.

Our new home—the total story of building a sod house, from the raw sod in the buffalo wallow to the completed structure plastered with native lime

After our crowded winter in what might be called Grant's duplex—because it was built half on his land, half on Mother's—we were eager to start work on a home of our own. It would be built clearly located on our own homestead so there could be no questions about its legality when it came time to prove up and claim our title. Our lack of experience was almost total except for what Grant acquired constructing his own soddy the previous year, but we went ahead and picked the location. During the summer, when the elder boys could best be spared from tending crops, we began the job by gathering the raw material.

Because of its generally flat surface, the land on which we had settled was covered almost entirely with buffalo grass. In the spring when the snow had melted off, or when there were heavy rains, the excess moisture gathered in the low-lying spots and stayed there until the hot summer sun evaporated it. As this vital supply of water receded, the wise buffalo pawed the mud away from the center of the pool, making a basin to store up the very last drop as it oozed from the mud. Year after year this process went on until there were several good-sized water holes, or buffalo wallows, on our land.* The strongest and best buffalo grass grew in these saucer-shaped dents, which were usually three or four feet in depth and from fifty to two hundred feet across. Since the grass had grown where there was ample moisture at least part of the spring, and enough in summer to nourish the roots, the sod thus built up was tough, well set in consistency, and easy to handle when cut. This was the sod that we used in building our house.

Even in those primitive days every farm had to have a breaking plow and a stirring plow. The former was for turning over the virgin soil and the latter for re-plowing after the soil had rotted and the first crop had been made from it. Except for special work now and then, the breaking plow retired from farm activity after the first year or so, and the stirring plow, cultivator, and disc took over. The breaking plow had an elongated molding board which by virtue of its peculiar shape gave the cut sod a neat little flip and landed it grass side down in the adjoining furrow. The plow had a pair of steel clips on the end of its tongue, and in each side of this double clip were four holes, one above the other. The depth of the plow penetration was set by hooking the clevis of the doubletree into any one of these holes. The lower you set the clevis, the higher it raised the point of the plow lay; and the shallower the cut, the thinner would be the layer of sod. A higher setting of the clevis, of course, would create just the opposite result. The cutter, or coulter as educated folk called it, ran along

* "Buffalo wallows are not made as Charley thinks but much more instinctively. Buffaloes had very delicate, sensitive skins under that mat of wool, and the great swarms of almost microscopic gnats drove them crazy. At the first swarming the buffaloes hit for any cooling mud, wallowed in it. The mud stuck in great lumps to the wool and protected the delicate skin under it, as well as smothering the gnats. Thousands of buffaloes wallowing in these holes made them deeper and deeper as the mud was taken out on the wool."— *Mari Sandoz*

to the left of the plow bottom, and this also could be adjusted to right or left to increase or decrease the width of the cut sod.

In our work we fixed the thickness of each piece of sod at approximately three inches, and its width at one foot. Brother Grant, using the best horses we had for the purpose, turned over the tough buffalo grass with his plow as neatly as those girls I later saw in the window of Childs Restaurant used to flip pancakes. When a goodly supply of sod had been turned over and allowed to dry awhile, the long, even furrows were cut crosswise into two-and-a-half foot lengths by means of the same rolling cutter removed from the plow and run across the flat sod. These pieces were then loaded on a flat wagon bed, grass side down, and hauled to the building site.

None of our family had any particular good taste or talent for artistic arrangement, but they did have that peculiar sense of precaution, a compound of common sense and foresight, which it seems so many pioneering folks are either born with or develop. The site selected for our home was located on a slight rise of ground, probably five feet higher than the surrounding terrain, which would provide good drainage. And when a road of sorts finally was made by the passage of wagon after wagon on the way to town, it turned out to be not over three hundred feet from our door. As we got more settled, we laid out our garden between this slowly developing road and the house, and even went to the trouble of creating a horseshoe curve. Supposing you were headed north, you could drive in on the south side of the garden, swing around past the house, and drive out to the main road along the north side of the garden. Pretty nifty, we thought.

After the site was selected, the ground was leveled off and the boundaries of each wall were set. The dimensions that the family had decided on were thirty-six feet long by twenty-four feet wide, with a half-high cellar house to extend out twelve feet from the west wall.* Grant had picked up a steel square somewhere, and using the sun as our guide we spotted the house almost exactly north and south and squared it with the east and west dimensions. Then the first course of sod was laid down and carefully tamped into place: this layer had an important role to play in supporting the completed structure. Each sod was put in place much as a brickmason would have done the job, except that no mortar was used. The sod pieces being cut as nearly as possible to 30" x 12" dimensions, it was quite simple to make one full round of base layer, placing each sod crosswise to the wall. Then the second layer was set in place with its longer side following the long way of the wall. And so the work proceeded until the walls were up to the desired height. I have no record of our progress, but it seems to me work had been going on less than two days when we started on the roof.

Along the level top of the side walls, about eight feet from the ground, we placed a straight, properly peeled pine log that had been brought down from the timber country. Then the gables were built up to the peak which would provide a roof slant of four or five feet. A bigger and stronger log, the ridgepole, was laid from the apex of one gable to the gable opposite, about thirty-six feet away. This pole was supported by a beam set midway of its length and well spotted on tamped soil at the bottom. Halfway between the ridgepole and the log on top of each wall was placed a smaller log, or pole, and with this skeleton framework in place we were ready for the roof to go on. But

---

* The half-high portion sat back four feet from the rest of the front, which gave us room for the swill barrel, sunk to half its height in the ground. With its cover on, we could easily hop on top it, then leap to the sloping roof of the cellar house, and thence to the roof of the main house to see if "Maw was a-coming home from town." —Author's note

first came the shaving-down job to make everything neat and give it a finished look. Wielded by Grant, a sharp hay knife—it has a keen, jagged edge and looks something like the picture of a lightning bolt—soon made both sides of our newly laid sod walls almost as smooth as brick.

Now we had the shell of a house with eight-foot walls and a total height of over twelve feet at the center of the roof. In the south wall was the main door and a small window to the left, as you faced front. As you walked north along the east wall there was a bay window—a delight to all who visited us as it provided a place for a lot of flowering plants. Because of the thickness of the walls and the projection of the windows, Mother could easily protect her blossoms during the coldest weather. Further north there was a side door which we seldom used except for ventilation on hot summer nights. Then came a side window and in the rear another window. There were no openings of any kind in the west wall excepting the one down into the cellar house. When the dirt had been taken out of this cellar-house annex, we had a fine place to keep our milk, butter, eggs, vegetables, etc. cool in the summer and just warm enough in the winter to prevent freezing. Its walls rose about four feet above ground level and with the cellar dug out five feet more there was plenty of head room as well as plenty of storage space.

In making the roof we used the cheapest boards we could find. These were laid down much as they would be in a frame house today—first nailed to the top at the ridgepole, then again at the center member, and finally to the log on top of the wall. Over this roof-sheeting we rolled tar paper, and then came the sod, placed grass side up. After each piece of sod was fitted snugly against its neighbor, the tiny cracks were filled with loose dirt and tamped down. In all the years we lived there, that roof never leaked a drop.

Nature having been good to this country, we soon found

a deposit of raw lime in the range of low hills west of us. This was not real lime like builders use, but related to it about as lignite is related to coal. Being more like magnesia or talc, it was none too strong, but when mixed with water and a little sand it could be applied to sod walls and give good service. After this native plaster had gone on to our inside walls, we had a very good-looking interior. We were to find that the plaster did rub off easily, but this was a small drawback for a product that was free.

Next, a wood floor was laid, and this gave us a great deal of pride and satisfaction, it being the only one in that section of the country. All our neighbors had dirt floors, which meant they had plenty of fleas also. Because of our fine floor, our home became the mecca for square dances and many were held there over the years.

With floor, roofs, and walls completed, we built a board partition across the house midway between the ends. There was a door in this dividing wall, and the rest of it provided a back for the long bench placed before the table where we sat at mealtime and playtime. Mother covered the rough wallboards with a run of cheese cloth over which she pasted bright-colored (though very cheap) wallpaper. You could tell how fast we children were growing by checking the grease spots where our heads rubbed on the wallpaper back of the bench. The spots were caused by some of us being remiss in the care of our hair and from the older boys being too free in applying bergamont and lard—the hair-dressing preferred by nine out of ten well-dressed pioneers.

The rear half of the house was our bedroom, and contained the collection of beds occupied by the various members of the family. In an attempt at privacy we strung wires and hung calico curtains between the beds. More substantial partitions would not have been feasible in so small a space, and besides that on winter nights, with the windows nailed shut and carpet rags stuffed in the door cracks, we wanted all the available air to circulate as freely as possible.

In the southwest corner of the front room, the boys boarded off a small space which Mother called the buttery —where she picked up that word is a mystery—and here were kept foodstuffs that didn't require the coolness of the cellar house. When our old cookstove was put in place near the west side of the living room—which was also cooking, eating, visiting, and conference room—we were all set for real "gracious living" as never before. In the winter, the addition of the big wood-burning heater on the east side of the room made everything nice and cozy regardless of the weather.

Our well, which we had dug later on, was about twenty-five feet to the southwest of our front door, and we built our granary about fifty feet from the well. Constructed of good solid lumber and set up on three-foot stilts to discourage rats and other pests, it was of generous size and well arranged as to bins and compartments for the safe storage of our crops. Back of the granary and a little to the north we built a substantial sod stable for the work horses and milk cows.

Further to the northwest we set up a portable straw stable for our younger stock and for cows not fresh (not giving milk). This rather unusual structure was purely seasonal; it was built crib style out of poles, posts, and willow branches interwoven to create a basket effect. The outer and inner walls were five feet apart, and when we threshed in the fall the machine was placed so that the straw carrier spurted straw all over the skeleton building. This was tamped down between the wall members, and when a door had been fitted between two posts provided for this purpose, our stock had a safe, sweet-smelling, cozy shelter through the long winter. The only bad feature was that the occupants kept munching away on the material out of which their stable was constructed, so in the end we could truthfully say they "ate themselves out of house and home."

If you add a sizeable sod henhouse twenty-five feet east of the straw barn and round off the scene with the proverbial Chic Sales specialty—or outhouse, or privy, or whatever name you prefer to designate this pipeless, unsanitary necessity—you will have the complete picture of where we lived, and how we built what we lived in, in the early days of our residence in Sheridan County.

When we decided to have a well dug, the job was done by Chris Burki—the man who gave us the news about the loss of our household goods the night we arrived.

In those days well-digging was all done by hand, with spade and shovel, dirt bucket and windlass. You started with a goodly supply of two-by-fours for the corner supports and plenty of board lumber for the side walls. A two-by-four was put up at each of the four corners of the well opening, which was usually three feet square. As the dirt was dug out and disposed of, the corner posts slowly traveled down and side boards were set between them. When the hole got down below shoveling depth, the dirt was loaded into a carrying bucket, which was made by sawing a heavy barrel in half and adding a number of reinforcing hoops. The bucket was attached to a heavy rope and hauled to the top by a windlass. Then the dirt was dumped out, and down went the bucket again.

Of course all this digging and dumping simply provided entertainment for me, as I was far too young to take any useful part in the proceedings. However, when the well got down somewhere around a hundred feet I engineered a diversion which did nothing to help things along and might have ended seriously.

A large colony of blackbirds had gathered nearby, no doubt attracted by the smell of fresh, moist earth—if a bird can smell. These were not the ordinary drab-colored birds usually found around barnyards, but handsome red and gold fellows mighty pretty to behold. One afternoon there were probably twenty-five of these beauties sitting on the top wire of the barbed-wire fence that ran near the well. Seeing this row of big, fat, juicy birds, it occurred to me that here was the makings of a grand dish for supper. I sneaked out past the granary, picked up an endgate rod, and moved back within striking distance of the fence. Then with all my might I let go *wham* on the top wire, and in an instant the air was filled with fussing and feathers. It looked like I'd killed them all; but soon the effects of the shock wore off and most of the birds flew away, apparently not seriously hurt.

Out of all this commotion I managed to pick up a total of one bird—not enough for a good pot pie. So I got the bright idea of sending him down to Chris in the well. (I had not yet been exposed to Swinton's Second and Third Grade Reader, which would have informed me that a pound weight falling vertically will travel 32 feet the first second, 64 the next, and 128 the third.) Since the well was now around a hundred feet deep, you know that my bird must have been going some when Chris heard the swish of air and the fluttering of outspread wings, and looked up just in time to get claws, feathers, and bill smack in the face. To quote his earlier words to us, he was sure in a helluva fix. It dawned on me that I would be too, if I didn't flee from the wrath to come—and at the rate he was sur- facing it was coming fast.

From my hiding place near the granary I could see Chris's face, and if I hadn't been scared before, I would have been then. But after he'd washed up it didn't look so bad, and apparently he didn't feel so bad either because be- fore long he went back down.

In another day or so the well was finished at 134 feet. It gave fine soft water, very cool and satisfying when we came in from harvesting or threshing, or took a gunny-sack-wrapped jug of it to the fields for our refreshment there.

Like David of old, I sometimes yearn for a drink from that well, no doubt long ago filled up and forgotten.   •

Our daily bread: what we ate and how we got it, and how we made use of many of the weeds that grew so prolifically

Ever since the Divine Creator set the Universe spinning, man has depended on the good earth for his food, his raiment, and his equipment; and on our Sheridan County farm we certainly did find it the only source of things to keep soul and body together. Mother Nature, not a scientist with a test tube, originated the food we put on our table. The sunshine and rain produced the green grass which the cows ate and from which they created milk—the best fluid nourishment ever found—as well as butter to eat or sell. Our hogs gave us meat and lard, both indispensable to farm living. Out of a butchered hog we got fresh ham, salted-down side meat for later use, a meal or two of liver, and—some years—head-cheese. (Somehow or other we never learned the art of sausage-making, and the one time I tried smoking a ham I not only scorched the ham badly but almost burned down the part of our house that was burnable.)

From our fields we gathered corn, wheat, oats, and rye. The corn went for feed except some we took to Rushville to be ground into meal, and from which we made mush for mush-and-milk at night and fried mush with " 'lasses" the next morning. We sold our wheat, but now and then Mother would parch a batch to mix with coffee beans to make that item last longer; and we sometimes parched corn as a delicacy. Oats had only two uses: as feed for the horses and as a covering for salt pork after it had been brined and dried out and was ready to be packed away. It could be kept reasonably air-tight under a foot or two of clean, dry oats out in our granary.

Potatoes, turnips, rutabagas, squash, and pumpkins all found their places in our daily diet, both in season and for as long after as they could be kept fit to eat. What we no longer found edible was always mighty welcome to the hogs or milk cows.

During the summer months, weeds contributed much to our table. As in most countries, weeds—vegetables out of place, as some people call them—grew in profusion, creating lots of problems and entailing lots of work in their eradication or control. But in the O'Kieffe home, our slogan was: "If you can't beat'em, eat'em."

The names of three of these helpful little pests come to my mind as I write: pigweed, lambsquarters, and pussley. Where the folks got such a word as "pussley" is beyond me: it couldn't be a corruption of parsley because this weed did not resemble parsley any more than I look like Einstein. But that's what everybody called it, so there must have been a reason for its name.* Mother had a way of slipping a small hunk of salt pork in the pot with the cooking weeds and, brother, that made the difference.

Thus did Mother Earth give us in some form or other our daily bread for which we were most truly thankful, even though there was never any grace said before or after meals in our home. Maybe it was because we didn't have

---

* Pussley is one of several common names for purslane (*Portulaca oleracea* L.). Others are: pursley, wild portulaca, and duckweed. Pigweed (*Amaranthus hybridus* L.) is also known as red root and green amaranth. Lambsquarters (*Chenopodium album* L.)—sometimes called pigweed, too—is commonly known as white goosefoot or meal weed. —*Editor's note*

the time and maybe we didn't have the inclination, but I think mostly we just plain didn't know that such things should be done.

Since those days of long ago I have eaten collards in the Deep South and mustard greens in Kentucky, to say nothing of lobsters in Maine, oysters in the many bars in New Orleans, and broiled Spanish mackerel in Gulfport, Mississippi, but none of their dishes tasted any better than did the weeds of Northwestern Nebraska back in the 1880's. Why? Because I was hungry then as I have never been hungry since.

Speaking of operations: the art of hog-butchering and chicken-killing

Among the many workaday chores most young men had to learn was the messy but necessary job of butchering. This was how you got your diploma:

First, you honed the family butcher knife to razor-edge sharpness; next, the victim was brought to the scene of operations and the scalding barrel filled. Then came the big moment: you had to plunge the knife into the porker's throat at just the right spot and at just the right angle so that the point would enter his heart. When this was done properly, the hog would stagger about for a minute and then drop dead. Now you grasped him by his hind feet and soused him repeatedly into scalding water, the scalding barrel being set at an angle so the carcass could be pulled out and shoved back with the greatest possible ease. When the hair had been sufficiently loosened up, you then scraped him entirely free of it. Usually this was done with a very sharp corn knife—an implement which, because of its length and fine steel, could be used for a variety of other things than cutting corn fodder.*

After he got his clean shave, the hog was prepared for the gallows and last rites. A slit was made in each hind leg just a little above the hoof, and the strong sinew found there was spread away from the leg to make an opening into which the end of the gambrel was inserted. Made of strong wood usually salvaged from a broken or worn-out singletree, the gambrel was long enough to spread the hind legs wide and strong enough to hold the heaviest hog. It was hooked over the end of an elevated pole or wagon tongue, thus raising the carcass off the ground for evisceration. (Gutting was our word for it.)

Almost anyone could carry out the final phases of butchering—cutting up the carcass and putting away the hams, shoulders, side meat, etc. Some of the meat would be smoked if facilities were available, or salted down and stored, or given to neighbors on a lend-lease basis. Because cash money was scarce, I do not recall of any sales being made, although trading and outright gifts were very common. If a butchered animal was to be sold, it had to be hauled to town and there disposed of for some cash and the rest in trade.

While the young man in the family was taking his lessons in butchering and other branches of animal husbandry, his sister or girl friend was getting used to, and learning the knack of, chopping off the head of some ancient rooster or

---

* "In sticking a hog the art is in sticking him so he bleeds very fast before he dies, or the flesh will be full of blood, hard to keep because blood spoils very readily and the meat is neither tasty nor the pale silvery color of good pork. The trick is to stick the pig not in the heart, which kills him immediately, with no bleeding worth the word, but in the aorta, the large vessel *at* the heart. Then the blood gushes forth as the pig kicks his last, not dying for a half minute or so, and then from loss of blood. . . . When one end of the hog is scalded, it is turned and the other end scalded too, before the scraping. [Otherwise] he would have one end cold and hairy and needing what Charley calls it, a shave."—*Mari Sandoz*

an old biddy hen who had signed her own death warrant by falling down on egg-laying, her real mission in life. After decapitation with a sharp axe on the chopping block out by the wood pile, the victim was allowed to flop around for a minute or two, so as to complete the bleeding process. Then the fowl would be doused in scalding water to loosen its feathers, after which the larger, coarser ones would be plucked. Next, the young lady would find herself a fairly big piece of paper, set it afire on top of the stove, and rotate the plucked fowl in the flames at just the proper height to singe off the remaining feathers, especially the tiny pin-feathers that could not be removed by hand plucking.

After all the entrails were removed through a slit in the fowl's back door, the empty hull was washed out with cold water. Great care had to be taken to see that the gizzard was not cut or broken open and its contents scattered about in the chicken's body. The gizzard contains an assortment of items—bits of glass, grains of sand, small pieces of metal—which are useful in the living fowl's digestive process, but very destructive to the flavor of the cooked fowl. After the gizzard has been removed and the chicken split open and thoroughly cleaned, it (the gizzard) can safely be re-united with the rest of the fowl to be cooked in the manner best adapted to that particular bird and to the family's taste.

'Lasses-Makin' Time: a description of the crude machinery that was used in squeezing the cane stalks and boiling down the juice

During two or three of our years on the Sheridan County farm, we raised a pretty fair patch of sorghum cane. When the proper time came in the fall, before the first killing frost, we stripped off the leaves and cut off the bunch of seeds at the top: the leaves would be used as fodder and the seeds as feed—mainly for the chickens. They relished these seeds, which also made them better layers. Then we cut down the naked stalks and loaded them on the wagon.

Old Man Hardy had set up a sorghum mill on his farm which was two miles east of us on the way to the Lone Butte, and there we hauled our cane stalks. (He had to call his outfit a sorghum mill because his son Rufus was a school-teacher, and no common word like " 'lasses" would do in that family.) The mill was a simple affair consisting of a pair of steel rollers much like a clothes wringer except the rollers were larger and were set upright, not horizontally. As the canes were fed into them, they were rotated by a set of gears powered by an old horse hitched to a long sweep, which he pulled around and around in an endless circle.

The cane juice thus crushed out dropped down into a receptacle which was emptied at frequent intervals into the nearby cooking tank. This was made of galvanized sheet metal, and was six feet long by four feet wide and about ten inches deep. Below the tank was the firebox, which was stoked with every sort of heat-making material that could be found around the farm. The yellowish-green scum was skimmed off the top several times, and then the fully cooked molasses was drained off ready to be taken home in what-ever type of container we could round up. As I recall, for his toil Old Man Hardy kept one gallon out of every four.

At home the molasses was stored away for winter use—and did it ever taste good! Maybe a bit strong for our tastes today, but it sure went well on breakfast pancakes, and we also mixed it with lard to make a spread for Mother's home-made bread. Altogether, it was a mighty big reward for planting an acre or so of cane and cultivating it along with the adjoining corn.

If we had only known about it, what wonderful taffy and

other kinds of candy we might have made from our home-grown 'lasses. But what you don't know doesn't hurt you, so we never missed such treats.

Vessels of honor and dishonor: an account of the shortage of things to put things in, as compared with today's abundant supply of all such items

In these days when you can buy practically everything you may want in the way of food neatly put up in usable bowls or glasses or plastic cartons, it may be a bit hard to appreciate the difficulty we had in securing containers for any item we had to keep in our home.

When we had to buy lard between butcherings we could get it in twenty-five-cent, fifty-cent, or dollar quantities, hence the common designations—"quarter lard bucket, half-dollar lard bucket, dollar lard bucket." These tin jewels usually found their way to the schoolhouse, each family using the size which corresponded to the number of its children. I lived too close to the school to carry my dinner, so the lard buckets we obtained from time to time served in a variety of ways. As well as being useful in the kitchen, they came in particularly handy when we went down across the Niobrara River to pick serviceberries.

But it was the 31-gallon coal-oil barrel that the average family would almost commit murder to get. Since these were returnable to the dealer we had to pay at least as much for one as the merchant would get in credit for it, so it was a big day when we acquired a coal-oil barrel. Before putting it in use, we set fire to the barrel's interior to burn out the oil residue and also to coat it with charcoal, thus preventing premature rotting of the wood. A barrel might start its career by catching rain water that ran off the granary roof (if and when it ever rained). After that, it might serve as a scalding barrel during hog-butchering. And finally, when the staves and hoops grew old and it threatened to spring a leak, it would be sunk halfway in the ground and end up as our swill barrel.

One of the most useful containers that was ours merely for the price of its contents was the baking-powder can. Either the lid or the can itself was just the right size for a biscuit cutter, and for years we lived on biscuits neatly cut out by Mother with a baking-powder can lid.

Since there were no jugs or pitchers then except as part of a store-bought kitchen set, we would have gone wild with joy if we'd been able to get our hands on any of today's vacuum-packed two-pound coffee containers. (Only where would we have gotten the $1.89 to pay for two pounds of coffee?) We bought what coffee we could afford in one-pound packages made of medium-heavy waxed paper. A two-pound package cost twenty-five cents, and they threw in a pretty bird picture in color so that you might be induced to keep on buying Arbuckle's Ariosa or McLaughlin's XXXX until you had pictures of all the known birds of the world.

For our milk we used wide, shallow tin pans, each capable of holding at least a half gallon. These were placed flat on the dirt floor of the cellar house where the milk kept nice and cool. After the cream rose to the top it was skimmed off and later churned and made into butter, which we sold at the store for enough to buy what food we didn't raise. Our churn was the standard model of the day—the body of some kind of crockery and a dasher of wood that you worked up and down through a lid with a hole in its center. Every so often you would raise the dasher and inspect the mess that had gathered on its surface. If this looked right, the churning was about done and the butter "made," as we said then. The butter was packed in a tall earthen jar, or crock, and stored until we had enough to take or send into town.

Among the vessels of dishonor were, of course, the little yellow ones with handles that stayed coyly under our beds waiting to be pulled out on cold or stormy nights when it was neither practical nor desirable to go scurrying out to the rustic roost in back. We also had the slop bucket, or swill pail, which had the lowly job of transporting malodorous refuse from the swill barrel at the side of the house to the trough in the hog pen some distance away.

Each one of our heterogeneous fleet of vessels did its work as best it could during its rather protean existence. They weren't very pretty and not always efficient, but we managed to get along together and at times really enjoyed each other's company.

Sheridan County Flora including Tumblin' Weeds—
the most complete account of this pest
that has ever been written

As the West became more thickly settled, the native Fauna began to disappear; but most of the Flora remained to delight and serve us all. There were the native grasses like the bluestem, slough grass near the water pools or lakes, the buffalo grass, and bunch grass. And of course there were weeds of every sort, some harmful and very undesirable, others good to eat. But it was in the field of flowers that this section was most wonderfully blessed. Not that a hungry person could eat them, but they did a lot to give color and cheer to an otherwise rather drab and flat landscape. In many cases, too, the most beautiful flowers eventually yielded to tasty and much sought-after fruit. In those days of scanty living we really did believe that beauty is as beauty does, so it was the tree, bush, or plant which gave us food that we regarded as most beautiful and interesting.

Many of our wild fruits were related to and named after their domesticated cousins—for instance, red and blue plums, wild grapes, chokecherries, and currants both yellow and blue. These could be found in almost every section along or near the Niobrara River. But the two most remarkable fruits, the likes of which I have never found anywhere else, were the sand cherry and the buffalo berry.

In its body composition the sand cherry is fibrous, made up of the same vegetable growth as a cherry tree, but instead of growing upward it sprawls out more like a vine. As it nearly always lives in the vicinity of an actual or potential blowout,* there are times when this unusual plant is entirely covered with sand. Nevertheless, it keeps right on growing, and many a time have I pulled on one sand cherry only to pull the rest of the plant out of the loose sand with a dozen or two big luscious berries attached to the branch on which I thought there was but one. The fruit itself is about the same size as a Bing cherry, and is just as beautiful and inviting to look at, but it is puckery to the taste and except when dead-ripe has to be treated before it is edible.

We gathered them by the washtub-full at picking time, and took them home where they were pitted by Mother and Minnie, and then dried in the bright sun until they looked quite like small scraps of chamois skin that had become soiled by handling. While I do not recall having eaten any chamois skin, I think it must taste something like these dried bits of sand cherry. But times Mother had gotten a little extra trade value out of her butter and eggs at the Rushville store, she would bring home a small lot of dried apples, and when five or six of these were added to a gallon

---

* A crater scooped out by the wind. See page 161.—*Editor's note*

of the dried sand cherries we children ate them gladly to get the apples.

The buffalo berry almost defies description both as to its growing habits and the fruit it produces The trees—or rather large bushes—were none too plentiful and when the berries were ready for picking there was likely to be plenty of competition. Usually found along the Niobrara River, these shrubs had such an odd color and shape that they could be easily spotted by anyone who knew what to look for. The gray, almost white, leaves were long and narrow, much like the leaves of the better grade of China tea. The bushes themselves were thorned, like some plum trees, but the fruit itself was small, brilliant red, and very acid. It clung to the mother bush as long as possible, and the best time to gather these berries was right after the first frost. You harvested them by spreading a sheet around under the bush and beating the branches until the fruit fell off into it. Generally the in-gathering was none too plentiful, but what we got was well worth the labor.

Those of us who could dig up enough sugar made jelly out of the bulk of our berries, saving a few for sauce. Made without any modern pectin ingredients, buffalo-berry jelly was very transparent and could almost pass the old test for clarity—being able to read a newspaper through a glass of it. We had no newspaper to make the test with, but this didn't stop us from enjoying and admiring the jelly. There may be a domesticated buffalo berry now, but I have never found one in any seed catalog that bore any resemblance to the wild buffalo berry.

I could not write about our Flora without saying some nice words about the "sarvisberry." * Where the mixed-up

---

* It has been suggested that just as the word "vermin" became "varmint" in dialect, so "serviceberry" came to be pronounced "sarvisberry." Both the serviceberry (*Amelanchier canadensis* [L.] Medic.) and the buffalo berry (*Shepherdia argentea* [Nutt.]) are found else-

races of mankind who made up the early settlers of the West got this word I have no idea, but I do know where and when we found the berries, and how delicious they were. In general, they were quite like the blueberry. Starting out as green, they turned red and finally a rich almost transparent blue. At the outer end of each berry were three little leaves. Their habitat was along the lower slope of the hills just south of the Niobrara and before you reached the actual sandhills—there they did not seem to do so well. The shrub grew to varying heights, but was never so tall that it was any problem to pick the fruit. In fact, the serviceberry was about the easiest of all berries to find if you knew where it grew, and the most suitable for eating after you had picked it—rich and mellow, sweet but not sickeningly so, meaty and not too juicy, and just plain perfect whether fresh with cream, stewed into sauce, or baked in pie.

With a few minor exceptions, this covers the edible Flora in our locality. Then there were the weeds we used for greens and hog feed, which I have already told about; the notorious tumblin' weed; and cactus.

According to those who have received a reasonable amount of education, when one cactus meets another cactus you must call them cacti. But what they were called was something I didn't worry about. My worry was whether or not I would step on one as I bounded over the prairie in search of something or just to bring in the cows. Regardless of size, type, or correct botanical name, they all had spines and they all hurt—especially in the early spring before my winter-coddled feet had developed rhinoceros-hide protection. There are said to be as many as 150 varieties of cactus in our land today, but I have run across

where, but the author is correct in saying that the sand cherry (*Prunus besseyi* Bailey) is endemic to the Sandhills region.—*Editor's note*

—and I do mean run across—only three or four in my ramblings around the buffalo-grass country.

There was the ball cactus [*Mamillaria vivipara* (Nutt.) Haw.], looking much like a small pincushion full of pins with their points sticking out at you, and, in this same general class, the clump type, which was made up of a whole collection of little pincushions. At times the larger clumps reached a diameter of six to eight inches. Both types grew squat on the ground and were pretty hard to locate until it was too late.

Another variety [*Opuntia humifusa* RaF.] commonly encountered was made up of several flat discs attached to the parent plant in a way that made them look like a display of king-size all-day-suckers. Each disc was well sprinkled with long and very sharp spines or thorns; but because it was easily spotted it was more of a nuisance to animals than to people. Sheep, in particular, would get a goodly supply of these spines embedded in their noses and serious infection could result. I know this to be a fact because I herded about a thousand sheep the autumn of 1896, and our favorite Sunday morning chore was to catch a hundred or so of the worst affected and wash their noses out with a carbolic acid solution. I was not interested in the church then, and it seemed as good a way as another to start the Sabbath day.

My rather limited reference library informs me that unlikely as it seems the rollicking, good-for-nothing tumblin' weed is a cousin of the amaranth, one of our most decent and lovely flowering plants. The encyclopedia also says that the tumbleweed is found in the prairie regions—and that statement I can certainly go along with. The weeds grow out there in superabundance—or anyway they did in Sheridan County between 1886 and 1898, and I bet they are still there.

Now none of us regards very highly the man who grows

rich from the soil or natural resources of one section of our country, and then moves away to spend his wealth somewhere else. Probably this is why you will find very few, if any, folks who will admit that the tumblin' weed has any excuse to live. He saps up the precious water supply from the soil with his thirsty roots, and avidly consumes every atom of plant food within his reach. Then when he has become fat and sassy away he rolls to parts unknown, never to return. And does he roll! With a sixty-mile-an-hour Northwestern Nebraska wind at his tail, he covers the ground so fast that a top cowhand on the fleetest broncho ever put to saddle hasn't a chance of keeping up, much less overtaking him. The tumbleweed is built for traveling, and old Nebraska used to be able to provide all the propelling power he could possibly demand. Although born and reared in Western Nebraska, given a good breeze and with no fences or ravines to stop him, in a day or so he'll be all ready to settle down in Missouri.

Borrowing a word or two from the Bible: Unto what shall we liken the tumbleweed? It has some green and red in its foliage combination, but in most ways it resembles no other plant. Built rather squatty, it grows to be much more massive or bulky than most weeds, often reaching a diameter of three feet. Its roots are above the ground, gathered in a tight little cluster in the center of the plant, and the foliage is quite densely put together. Hugging the earth as it does, nothing could possibly grow under its umbrella-like body. Usually the tumbleweed is found along the edge of cultivated fields where the tilled soil meets the grassland. There does not seem to be enough open soil between the roots of the prairie grass to permit seed lodgement.

The tumbleweed becomes a migrant in its adult year. The weeds that grew on our farm sprang from seeds dropped there by a roving parent who had grown to mature tumbleweedhood during the previous season, probably a hundred miles to the northwest. Our local-grown crop would be cast to the wings of a wind which would take it rolling along in the general direction of the southeast. This process of propagation and migration continues until they run out of seeds, wind, or friendly soil; and you will find few of these pestiferous weeds east of the Missouri River or south of Iowa.

Aside from their soil-robbing, moisture-stealing characteristics, tumbleweeds cause lots of trouble by piling up in huge masses against fences or buildings. Sometimes the wind may dump tons of them into ravines or gorges where, being quite dried out in the course of their trip, they create a fire hazard. In blizzards these huge piles of vegetable growth may be blanketed by snow, masking the presence of the ravine and thus turning it into a death trap for cattle headed that way. In the past, many ranchmen have lost heavily from this cause alone.

So you can see why the tumblin' weed has no friends out where he is born, and is received with ill will when he arrives in some other state. It may or may not be significant that even before I left Northwestern Nebraska the "Communist" branch of the tumbleweed family moved in and took over; and in a short time what we had called tumbleweeds were known as Russian thistles.*

---

* "Tumbleweeds and Russian thistles are not the same, although both are often called tumbleweeds. The true tumbleweed is spicy in odor and spineless, light green until frost and then turning a handsome purplish red. Russian thistles are darker, can grow to around five, six feet across, turn brownish red in the fall before breaking loose to tumble in the wind and, ripe, are very spiny, stickery. They take whole fields if permitted, while the true tumbleweed usually remains at the edges looking in."—*Mari Sandoz*

*Sheridan County Fauna, with particular attention
to the prairie dog*

Now as to Fauna of this part of our country. Of course the advance of civilization and the settlement of the land meant death or deportation for the buffalo and shortly after we arrived in 1884 the antelope went the same way. I recall with a pang the morning I climbed up to the roof of our sod house and saw my last drove of antelope scampering across the corner of our farm, about a half mile to the northwest. They were most graceful and good to see, and I have no doubt that their flesh made mighty good eating. But I never tasted such luxuries then nor have I to this day had a bite of venison, buffalo, or bear meat.

Although the big animals were gone there were plenty of smaller ones left behind, including the predatory ones and lively little troublemakers like the pocket gopher and the ground squirrel. We also had the cottontail and his more grown-up cousin in the nearby timber section, and of course the ubiquitous jack rabbit without which there could hardly be a story of the West. But while he may be a nuisance, in those early days he filled many an empty belly when it sorely needed filling. Completing the roster of this group were the badger and a distant relative the local folk called the swift; and, inevitably, the skunk.

Since I will be telling about this fellow in connection with an occasion when he made a male wallflower out of me, I will pass on at once to a far more congenial little creature, the prairie dog. After many years of observation I can testify that this old western friend is not only an engineer, an architect, and a town planner, but also a sanitation expert and hydraulic engineer *par excellence*. On the side he is an acrobat, a clever espionage agent, and a gifted actor.

I first began to get acquainted with prairie-dog habits the day I decided to get myself enough pelts to make at least a pair of gauntlet mittens, if not an entire vest. I hitched our pony Maude to a stone-boat, or prairie sled, on which I had loaded the barrel that we used for scalding hogs. Then with my lunch and a bucket for dipping water out of the pond, and armed with a borrowed rifle, I set sail for the dog town about two miles from the farm. In the buffalo-grass country, a sled slides along on the grassy surface almost as easily as it would on snow or ice. The runners are made of small tree trunks with the bottom left rounded and the front ends sloped up to reduce friction. With just the empty barrel and myself aboard, Maude was able to trot right along and in a short while we were at the town site.

When a prairie dog picks out a town site, he is careful to see that the area offers the following advantages: ample room, usually at least forty acres; soil of just the right consistency to permit burrowing and yet firm enough to pack properly; water reasonably close by; and a terrain that will permit proper drainage—a very important factor in prairie-dog village life. You will seldom, if ever, find any rocks in or around a prairie-dog town.

The layout of the particular town I had come to was in all respects characteristic. The terrain was somewhat rolling, and in one corner of the village was a good-sized buffalo wallow which at this time of year was well filled with clear, clean rain water.

This was my initial attempt at prairie-dog hunting, so I had a lot to learn. While I scouted around for the best spot to operate from, the brave little fellows stood up and faced me with keen interest and loud shrill barks. They all seemed more curious than afraid. Soon I got what I was sure was a good target. I took careful aim at the clean white breast and fired. My bullet hit with a dull thud, and I thought I could see a spot of blood on his newly cleaned vest as he toppled over backwards. I was so sure I had bagged him that I turned part way around to get a shot at another. But when I glanced back I found that while my back was turned his pals had rushed out and hauled him into the nearest hole. So my first dog got away.

After many trials and misses, I finally bagged another and that is all I ever did get. Seeing that I was having such poor luck in shooting, I decided the thing to do was to drown them out. So I hitched Maude to the stone-boat, drove over to the pond, and filled the barrel with water. Then I drove her to what looked like the most logical hole and began pouring in the water. It rushed down with a gurgle, but as the hole did not seem to be filling up I went after another barrel and repeated the process. Still no results but the gurgle. After five barrels had been emptied in this one hole, I happened to look around and there, some hundred feet away, stood a big saucy prairie dog shaking the water off his back and no doubt grinning at my stupidity in thinking I could drown him out. All he had to do was retreat to one of the many archways of the interconnecting tunnels and let me keep on pouring till doomsday. The only water he'd gotten was the small amount that reached him before he could take off for his waterproof hideout.

Gathering up my one prize, I started for home full of disgust with myself as a prairie-dog catcher, and no less full of admiration for the smart little fellows who had planned so well and took care of themselves and each other so capably.

When for any reason a single hole in a prairie-dog town becomes unfit for use, the dogs abandon it, and it becomes the property of the owl or the snake. Many times have I seen these three kinds of creature, so unlike in every way, living in the same community. They don't fraternize in any way, neither do they fight each other: they merely coexist. But while the owl may serve as a sentinel to warn the dogs of approaching danger, what good the snake can do for the other two is beyond me. No doubt the rattler chooses the dog town because he respects the judgment of those who pick its location and lay out its intricate tunnel system. He also seems to know that the town authorities will keep everything spick and span, and there will be no stagnant water pools, no weeds or high grass, to interfere with his snakeship's vision or movements. In short, an ideal spot for a rattler to enjoy himself while someone else does all the work of preparation and policing.

The cultivation of the land as more people settled in our part of the country necessitated many moves for the prairie dog, and one of these was, to me, most interesting. During its first period of prosperity, Sheridan County started a very fine fair at Rushville, and there the folks built the finest kite-shaped track west of Red Oak, Iowa, then the racing capital of the West. But after a few years the crops began to fail and soon the Fair Grounds had to be sold under a foreclosed mortgage held by Old Man Musser, the Rushville banker. But there were no bidders and soon the prairie dogs took over. Here they found many things to their liking and as there was no way to discover how much tunneling they had done under the track, it was not considered safe ever to run horses on it again. So the prairie dogs accomplished what a lot of mind-other-people's-business committees are still trying vainly to do in other places: namely, they drove out racing.

Among the larger and more destructive wild animals in Sheridan County was the prairie, or gray, wolf, not infrequently seen along the tree-bordered Niobrara and now and then in the chophills that lead away from the stream. This wolf was big enough to fell a good-sized animal, and quite hard to track down and kill. There were still a few to be found in the more remote sections when I left that part of the country in 1898.

Then there was the coyote—and please say "ki-yoat" when you pronounce it. To my mind only a tenderfoot would pronounce the word "ki-yoty," and I doubt if the coyote himself would approve of it. Aside from my defense of his name, however, I refuse to stick up for this sneaky, skulking, treacherous devil. He is not only tricky and dishonest; he is downright deceitful. He will let out a mournful howl from a point to the south of your camp and in a flash he is sending up another howl from the north or west or east. A newcomer will be convinced that he is entirely surrounded by coyotes when actually there is but one doing all the howling.

This creature's greatest delight is to come across a steer or calf who has been weakened by illness or hunger; he can make an end of this poor helpless victim with little effort and no danger. In the early spring, at calving time, you will find the coyote lurking, stealthily watching for a winter-weakened cow to drop her calf and be lacking in the strength to defend it. This habit of the coyote's keeps cattle-owners on guard for at least two months every spring. When the season on weakened cows or feeble calves has ended, the coyote preys on chickens that have gotten too far away from their home yard. Occasionally, also, he is able to take a grouse or rabbit by surprise.

Still farther out on the fringes of civilization were to be found the bobcat, the black wolf, and the bear; but none of these were numerous enough to constitute a menace to either man or domestic animals. In the lakes and along some of the streams there were plenty of muskrats, mink, and—where timber was found—both beaver and otter.

Now we come to the birds I used to know. Chief among these I would list the meadow lark, a typical western bird.

From early spring until late fall, and from early morning till late afternoon, you will find one of these joyful fellows sitting atop almost every fence post, literally throwing his heart at the sky. His repertoire is not very extensive, but oh, it's cheerful on the ear of the farmer slowly driving by and to the lonely cowpoke riding the long stretches of fence.

Then there is the one we called the snowbird, a fine, plump little guy with a salt-and-pepper suit neatly fitted and worn with style. He usually was more active in the winter and at times was about the only sample of wild bird-life around the farm.

Around the water holes and nearby edges of farmed land, we found the noisy killdeer, the plover, a variety of edible snipe, and the wonder of them all, the curlew, who had a bill somewhat like the pelican's. It was about four inches in length and very much curved downward. The curlew had a plump body and was mighty good eatin'.

In the swamps, sitting astride a tall cattail where he could entertain the ranch hands mowing the hay close by, you would find the red-breasted blackbird and his yellow-winged cousin, the bobolink. The bobolink not only had an attractive personality and a sweet voice, but he had an odd-ball trait that was most fascinating. Every so often he would seemingly go berserk—fly straight up until he all but disappeared into the blue, then return to earth in a series of straight drops, each drop ending in a burst of song.*

One of my personal favorites was the mourning dove, a modestly beautiful little creature in his trim blue-gray. The

* "I never heard of a yellow-winged bird that could be called a bobolink. There's a fine yellow-winged blackbird who lived among the red-headed and red-winged ones. The bobolink Charley describes by action is a prairie bird, not a marsh liver—and is black with white on the wings as he soars high, spilling song all the way up and sloping down while his grayish-brown mate sits on the nest in some inconspicuous clump of grass. Bird experts often argue that there is no western bobolink, that this is a prairie bunting of some sort. We call them bobolinks."—*Mari Sandoz*

remarkable thing about him was his ability as a ventriloquist. His soft coo would come floating through the air to your ear as though it had started out as a much louder sound many feet away, while in reality the bird was giving out that coo not over a yard or so from where you were standing.

Simply because they were there, not because of any merit, I will conclude my list with two undesirables: the chicken hawk and the prairie-dog owl. The former was a real nuisance and the latter not worth a hoot—except, of course, to another owl.

I make no claim that this listing is complete, but it will give you some idea of the Fauna and the Flora native to our section of the country as it was being settled up and civilized. Incidentally, I have used the high-sounding words Flora and Fauna mainly to let people know that we did have Latin during the last year I spent in Rushville High School.

III

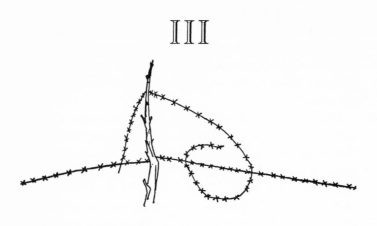

THE NEW LIFE

*Our farm community: a description of the people in
it and where they lived, and how we got along together*

CITY PEOPLE, when they talk about neighbors, usually
mean folks across the street or next door or maybe
even under the same roof, should they happen to make their
home in an apartment building. But in a farming or ranching area, although "neighbors" still refers to the people living closest, nearness is measured in terms of miles instead
of blocks. At the period we were living on our Sheridan
County homestead, seeing a neighbor—or seeing anybody,
as far as that goes—while not so unusual as to be a real novelty, was certainly not something that happened every day.
The men got together when they traded work on each
other's places, and of course the children went to school for
part of the year, and in an emergency, such as illness, a
neighbor woman might be called in. But aside from the

semimonthly gatherings during the winter, told about later on in this chapter, there was little social intermingling. Several times a year we did have dances at our home which were always well attended, drawing folks from across the Niobrara River to the south and halfway to Rushville on the north.

The Rushville-Gordon area did not begin to be settled up until 1883 and we got there the next year, so though not first-comers it would be correct to describe our family as early settlers. (I know of no hard-and-fast rule about this, but to my mind "early settlers" in our part of the county were the ones that got there before the railroad did.*) Before too long the O'Kieffe clan received reinforcements in the form of sister Belle and her husband Steve Auker, who moved out in the summer of 1886, and brother Ab, who joined us in 1887.

Others from Johnson County were our former neighbors the Wasmunds, who came out the same year as Belle and Steve and became neighbors again when they located to the southeast of our place. Old Man Wasmund, the father of our "stowaway" Charley Wasmund, quickly became a prominent figure in the community. He was outspoken and in his digging around had developed a better line of conversation than the mill run of folks out there. Confirming this is the fact that he was elected County Treasurer, holding office for two succeeding terms, and later on was elected County Commissioner. His oldest son, H.F. Junior—or Hank—followed in his footsteps and was also County Treasurer.

The McBrides, who lived about a mile from brother Grant's, were a bit outside our orbit of activity, especially the mother, always spoken of as Old Lady McBride. She was a religionist of the thoroughest kind and seldom went

---

* The Fremont, Elkhorn & Missouri Valley Railroad reached Gordon in 1885.—*Editor's note*

out excepting when the Baptist preacher held forth at the district school. Three daughters, Emma, Mamie, and Anna, attended school when I did, but their older son Les spent little time around where I could see him.

I have already mentioned the Hardy family, who had the mill where we took our cane to be processed out. The father was considered very honorable and his son Rufus was the best educated man in the community. Near them was August Lowe, generally called Gus, a very capable plasterer and bricklayer, who got work now and then as Gordon began to build up.

After we had been living on our homestead for some time, the Barnhardt family moved in to the north of our northeast corner and built a most elaborate house. This made the neighbors rather unhappy, but the Barnhardts soon petered out and eventually moved away. Their lovely place was bought for a song by one of the Wasmund boys, George as I now recall.

A Polish family, the Hinderas, lived across the road to the east of us. Albert Hindera was way above the average in education, having obtained it before he came to Sheridan County, and his wife Anna was refined and as neat as a pin. He had a good frame house with all the conveniences available and his farm was the show place of the entire township. Also, he had a high-grade bull which we made use of every year. Albert's nephew Johnnie lived with them, and he and I palled around quite a bit. Another member of the family was Felix Hindera, Albert's brother, who lived in Gordon, where he was the most popular clerk in the best clothing and haberdashery store in the county.

There were two Bohemian families in our vicinity—the Havliks, who lived over the ridge of hills to the west of us, and the Thiels, whose farm was at the northwest corner of our place. I have read and heard that in some parts of the state so-called "bohunks" and "polaks" were resented and treated as second-class citizens, but in our community the native-born had little time or reason for disliking those of foreign background. Only now and then when in town did I ever encounter any animosity between native-born and foreign-born, and it was always when one of each group had been drinking and finally decided to fight it out in the street.

In those days it seemed that every community had at least one smart aleck, one half-wit, and one nitwit. The smart aleck caused little or no trouble, although he may have been a bit tiresome at times, especially when he happened to stray off his range and get into more refined society. The half-wit was most likely to be blessed with a strong back to offset his weak mind, and for this reason was far too frequently made the butt of jokes that involved hard work. If there was a heavy hayrack to be taken off the wagon in preparation for some other job, the chances are that the half-wit would be goaded into doing it. Someone would pass the remark that he probably couldn't even lift one end of the rack, much less take the whole thing off and set it on the supporting scaffold at the side. Now if there was one thing the poor fellow had to be proud of it was his muscles, so—as the boys knew would happen—he would put his strong back under the rack, lift up one end until it rested on the wagon standards, then repeat the process at the other end, and in a few more seconds would have the rack where the boys wanted it. Thus the half-wit vindicated himself, the boys had foxed him, the job was done, and all concerned felt good about it.

The nitwit, then commonly called "idiot," was less tractable and hardly ever became the object of jokes or of impositions like the foregoing. Usually he was considered harmless, and was allowed to spend his days much as he liked. There being no place to put such boys—or girls—

each family did its best to care for its own, and to my knowledge no tragedy was ever caused by one of these under-developed folk. The nearest approach to such a thing happened on the ——— farm, some three miles east of us and not very far from where sister Belle and Steve lived after their arrival. As the details were told to us, Mrs. ——— had gone to Gordon to buy supplies, leaving her small baby at home in the care of the other children, among them a big, strapping, mentally deficient son. Something happened to distract the other children, and the feeble-minded boy took advantage of the situation. He got out the big dishpan and filled it with water, set it on the stove, and poked up the fire. When the water was scalding hot, he took the baby out of its crib and was just in the act of dousing it in the hot water when fortunately the mother returned. All the boy said by way of explanation was: "That's what you did to my pet rooster yesterday."

Whatever may have been the cause—manifold racial background, lack of even elementary education, absence of social life—the total effect can best be summed up by the word *crude*. Folks lived in crude homes, mostly soddies with here and there a dugout. Their household furnishings were crude as well as woefully inadequate. Nearly every item in the house, with the possible exception of a favorite rocking chair or bureau brought along on the trip west, was homemade out of native lumber with the accent on utility rather than beauty or grace.

Behavior was also crude and in ordinary speech crudest of all, especially between males of almost every age and classification. When talking about an older person, it was always "Old Man Hardy" or "Old Lady McBride," and even the long-winded hard-shell Baptist preacher, Reverend Horner, always was spoken of by those outside his limited flock as Old Man Horner. But when any of these men of rough exterior and unpolished manners addressed any woman, young or old, he always did so gently, respectfully, and with all the politeness he had been able to acquire.

In spite of their being obliged to perform rough tasks day after day, I never came across one young lady who had allowed herself to become common, vulgar, or immodest. On the contrary, they were all so ladylike that on Sunday evenings when it was time to do the milking and a young woman's boy friend went along to keep her company, she always took the time and precaution to pin on a homemade gadget that passed from one edge of her skirts around under her instep and was attached to the opposite edge of her dress. Having thus haltered both feet she could proceed with her milking in the utmost confidence that no male-critter could see her body above the ankles.

So far as I personally am concerned, I had no idea as to what any young lady concealed between her neck (usually hidden by a very high collar) and her ankles. This condition of blissful ignorance obtained until I was in school in Rushville and met Hattie, the town tomboy. But that belongs to another part of my story; and right now is the time to go into the "three R" part of my education as it began in the schoolhouse down the road from our homestead.

Fairview School, District 38

> Still sits the school house by the road,
>   A ragged beggar, sleeping.
> Around it still the sumachs grow
>   And blackberry vines are creeping.

The last time I saw my western alma mater, she was still a-sittin' and a-sunnin', although the nice white paint she displayed when first I entered her doors was peeling and fading. The sad part of the situation when I went there was that most of the families with children who should be attending Fairview School had given up the struggle against drought and moved back east to Indiana or Missouri. A few had even gone to Idaho, a state which was then pretty much in the spotlight.

Of course, a lot of Whittier's poem doesn't apply to my first Sheridan County schoolhouse, for example the line "Around it still the sumachs grow." There was nothing around the building except dirt, hard-packed by many a barefoot youngster in the fall and spring, and further trodden down by horses and cattle when school was not in session. The teacher's desk was not "Deep-scarred by raps official" because it was just a kitchen table, and his only official weapon was a pointer which he used to draw our attention to things on the blackboard. As for "jack-knife carved initials," these were mostly confined to the male unit of the two sanitary annexes, spotted well apart and located some seventy-five feet to the rear of the schoolhouse. "Battered seats and warped floor" also fails to apply because each family made and brought its own seats, so there was little mutilation of them; and the floor was so well coated with mud or dust or snow gobs that if it was warped it didn't show it.

Specifically, our schoolhouse was of frame construction, about thirty-six feet long and twenty-four feet wide, painted white, and had a neat little half-moon sign above the door reading DIST. 38. As none of our people had yet heard that frightening term *Fire Hazard*, there was only one door, and this plus three windows on each side were the sole openings to let fresh air in and stale air out. Fresh air was not felt to be important either.

To each side of the door were the nails on which the pupils hung their winter garments—boys on one side, girls

on the other. Nearby stood the water bucket with its community tin dipper. In the main part of the room were the
desks, arranged in two rows with a four-foot aisle in the
center. Right near the front desks was the huge wood-
burning stove which kept part of the children broiling and
the rest lukewarm to freezing. Fuel was made available by
civic-minded parents who remembered the school when
they made a trip to the Pine Ridge section for their own
wood supply.

The homemade desks, which each family brought when
starting its children to school, were built of native lumber
and, as the Psalmist said about man, were "fearfully and
wonderfully made." Like the community water bucket and
dipper, these seats and desks were meant to be shared—the
seat of one unit combined with the desk for the pupil in
back, which combined with the one in back of that, and so
on until you reached the rear wall. If the boy or girl
seated just ahead of you jiggled or moved about in any
way, the top of your desk likewise jiggled. But the surface
of the seats being rough and sliver-filled tended to make
the scholars cautious about sliding around on them, so we
didn't have very much desk-shaking trouble.

When I started at Fairview in the fall of 1886 at six and a
half years of age, I drew as my seatmate one Alexander
Gosch, a Bohemian immigrant, aged thirty-four. He was
trying hard to learn his ABC's in English, just as I would
soon be trying to master Swinton's Second Grade Reader,
and was so intent on making good in his studies that he
didn't bother me at all.

My first teacher was Charley Daugherty, who, like most
of those early-day teachers, was none too well trained. He
did a little farming on the side—had to, I guess, as the teacher's pay was usually $20.00 per month. However, most of
us were in our early stages of learning so any teacher who
could maintain order could do the job fairly well. Off and

on through several years I studied under three different teachers, with time out for a couple of semesters I attended the school in Rushville. After Daugherty came Rose Sweeney and then Emmett Rosecrans, whose genuine Spencerian penmanship is one of the most prized entries in my old autograph album.

When the teacher came to the door in the morning, at noon, and after each recess period and rang his bell, that meant school was to start or, as the natives said, "had tuk up." It was always "tuk up" and "let out." After the noisy youngsters had been somewhat quieted down, we usually sang a song or two. Our singing was from memory with some doing better than others on "Listen to the Mockingbird" or "My Darling Nellie Gray" and suchlike—nearly always one song with a sad tear-jerking verse or two. Then came roll call and the day began with reading lessons followed by arithmetic problems, which were sometimes worked out on the blackboard behind the teacher's desk. We always had spelling lessons, of course, and there was supposed to be a prize for the one who had the most "head marks" at the end of the term. A head mark was given to the last one on the floor after a whole row had been given words to spell and, having missed, were counted out. In rough-and-tumble country schools such as Fairview, where all ages were taught in the same room by the same teacher, there was nothing which corresponded to a present-day school curriculum: the famous three R's were considered both indispensable and adequate.

At recess and during the noon hour, we played games like Dare Base, Pom, Pom, Pullaway, or Drop the Handkerchief, and when there was snow we played Fox and Geese. The little tykes played simple games that suited their age, usually inside the schoolroom. One Old Cat was the favorite of us boys whenever we could find enough material to make a ball. This ball-making job was something of a community affair. One boy would dig up an old rubber heel from a discarded rubber boot, and we would cut this into a sphere as best we could with our limited supply of jack-knives. Then we took all the twine we had been able to collect and wound it around this rubber core. We found that the tongue of an old shoe made a very satisfactory cover, and the mother of one of the boys learned how to cut it out and sew it on. For a bat, we made out quite well by whittling down a discarded neckyoke from which the hardware had been removed. But it was not easy to come by this latter type of item because everything in the way of hardwood was almost as precious as diamonds. Even old pitchfork handles would be whittled down to make husking pegs, necessary at cornhusking time each fall.

Old Lone Butte, some two miles to the east, which was our landmark for so many years, was a great place for us kids to play Making Indian Signs, which we did on its top. A strange phenomenon: from right out of a level plain, without so much as a stone or pebble, rose this hundred-foot-high butte. Its top was heavily covered with slabs of limestone, the like of which was not found anywhere nearby.

Every so often on Friday afternoon we would have special programs to which the parents would come to see what progress their various children were making. At these exercises, pieces were spoken by those who had elocutionary talent—or thought they had—and of course we always had a spelling match. The test words were taken from Swinton, our school speller. (My school life began just after the era of McGuffey schoolbooks, which the old-timers still love to talk about.) I recall one page was captioned "A Tuff Enuff Lesson," and it sure was. It included such words as *rough, dough, enough,* and *slough* which might bother folks of today.

When it came to speaking pieces, Annie McBride was the

most interesting. The last delivery made by Annie went like this:

> Poor little butterfly,
> Dead on the walk,
> Take him up, Jane,
> With a violet stalk.
> In Mother's flower bed
> Make him a grave,
> Let the geraniums
> Over him wave.
> Rest, little Butterfly,
> In your nice bed,
> A rose at your feet
> And a stone at your head.

Before the last line had been uttered, Annie was on the run off the platform, a very frightened but happy little girl.

The Literary and Debating Society, with accent on the dee

In a community made up largely of sod houses and a sprinkling of dugouts, nearly all of them well filled with children, it was natural for most of the social, cultural, and religious activity to center in Fairview schoolhouse. Lots of things took place within those hornet-daubed walls, most of them in the winter. I do not recall ever finding the schoolhouse door locked—anyone could enter it at any time. (You see we had no vandals in those days—and supposing one had come along, what was there for him to vandalize? I suppose he could have chopped up the benches for fuel, but nothing like that ever happened.) The only thing that was not held in the schoolhouse were dances, because there was no room between and around the heavy desks for dancing, especially the active variety we did.

On several Sundays of the year Old Man Horner, as the unregenerate natives called him, would hold forth and preach to his flock of hard-shell Baptists. Once or twice a year the Catholics would have a service; there was no local priest, so one had to drive all the way down from Holy Rosary Mission at Pine Ridge. We also had Sunday School of a sort, with folks all the way from six to sixty in the same class. I can still close my eyes and hear Old Man Wasmund, who was the self-selected teacher, say to me after he had read a verse or two from the Bible: "Charley, what is your inter-pration of that?" I don't know why he picked on me, except the others in the group were more or less tongue-tied, too diffident to speak out their "inter-pration."

But it was the Literary and Debating Society that put the crowning touch to our cultural activities. The Society meetings alternated on Friday nights—one would be Literary and the next Dee-bate. Because we had so few books, anything which might be suitable for a number on the Literary program was eagerly sought after and preserved, and when a performer could not pick up a new piece somewhere he would give one he had "inherited." We had no sheet music or song sheets, so songs were learned by listening to someone else sing them; and as there were few musical instruments around, all singing was done unaccompanied. Some nights a number or two would be rendered by some fiddler with better than the mill run of talent; once in a blue moon, brother Ab would perform on his mouth organ; and now and then someone would give a selection on the jew's-harp.

On Dee-bate nights the older men and women took part, and some of them did quite well. Old Man Wasmund, by virtue of his standing in the community, was always the presiding officer, and after the question for debate had been selected, the folks would choose up sides. I can recall but one of the many subjects debated—"Resolved: that pursuit is better than possession." Never did find out who won —in fact, even to this day I do not know for sure which is better.

Thinking back on these somewhat uncouth affairs, I believe that they played a larger part in the development of our section of the country than anyone realized at the time.

As I mentioned above, our entire community was without a single piece of printed music—excepting maybe somebody had a copy of Gospel Hymns No. 1, 2, 3, or 4—and this meant that all music, whether vocal or instrumental, had to pass from person to person "live." When a song or poem was brought out west from Indiana or Pennsylvania, it had to be picked up and learned by a local resident before he or she could sing or play it at a gathering.

Most all of the songs that came our way were of the sad type—many no doubt being used to express the emotions of new settlers in a country that was none too attractive in its early stages. Just why a person would be moved to sing a ballad about President Garfield's assassination or the love affairs of a girl from Jefferson City is more than I can say; but here are a few of the words that linger in my memory after all these years.

> My name is Charles Guiteau,
> That name I'll never deny.
> I left my aged parents
> In sorrow for to die.

Then there was one that went something like this:

> In Jefferson City where I did dwell
> A butcher boy I loved so well.
> He courted me my heart away
> And now with me he will not stay.

Of course I can account for the strictly local songs that pictured the general atmosphere and conditions of our new country, as for example:

> Oh, the hinges are of leather
> And the windows have no glass
> While the roof it lets the howling blizzard in.
> And I hear the hungry coyote
> As he sneaks up through the grass
> 'Round my little old sod shanty on the claim.

And there was this one, popular during the long dry period that sent so many once-hopeful settlers back east to live with the wife's folks:

> Oh, Nebraska land, dear Nebraska land,
> As on thy highest hill I stand
> And look away across the plain
> Wondering will it ever rain
> Till Gabriel comes with trumpet sound
> And says the rain has passed around.

Then there was the famous "Cowboy's Lament," which has been so badly rewritten to fit the tastes of modern entertainment:

> Oh, bury me not on the lone prairie
> Where the wild coyote will howl o'er me,
> Where the sunbeams glance on my prairie grave ...

In its original form, this ballad truly expressed the loneliness of the prairies and the average cowboy's hankering to be laid to rest in a less dreary country when his final roundup had come. Its modern version suggests a far more scenic country where you might almost enjoy being buried if you were a movie or television star instead of a puncher riding the range in dust, in scorching heat, in wind-driven rain. Under such conditions I cannot imagine a man singing

> And when I die you can bury me
> 'Neath the Western sky on the lone prairie.

It makes quite a difference if you were actually there or if you were just putting rhyming words together in some Tin Pan Alley back east. A man talks more sensibly about things he has actually experienced.

As an outgrowth of crop failures in the new Western Nebraska country, golden California came in for a bit of musical publicity:

> Since times are so hard, I'll tell you, sweetheart,
> I've a mind to leave off my plow and my cart
> And away to California my journey I'll go
> For to better my fortune as other folks do.

To which the cautious wife replies:

> Dear husband, remember the land of delight
> Is surrounded by Indians who murder by night.
> Your house will be plundered and burned to the ground,
> And your wife and dear children be scattered around.

Each time a tune or vocal number passed from one person to another some changes would be made, and many words were dropped or mispronounced as it traveled about from mouth to ear. Then, too, there was the foreign-born fellow who came over here with a song in his native tongue, to which little by little he had added an English word. One such member was rendered now and then by a Swiss farmer, and to me it sounded like this:

Palta colta oxen, swartzy broon a coo
Gipfs me mein a fadder
Ven ich hei rot e doo.

He translated this to me as meaning that a pair of old oxen
and a black-and-brown cow would be given to the girl by
her father when she got married.

Brother Grant had one or two numbers that he sometimes sang when he was calling a square dance. One was
titled "The Juice of the Forbidden Fruit," and though there
were several verses I can recall only this much:

Jim Blaine and Bob Ford
Drank theirs from a gourd,
General Grant as he smoked a cheroot;
Lily Langtry, they say,
Had been led astray
By the juice of the forbidden fruit.

I could go on quite awhile along these lines, but I'm sure
you get the general idea. As to instrumental music there
was—as I said—very little of that except fiddle-playing. I do
not recall ever seeing a guitar until several years later in
Rushville. As with the songs, violin pieces had to be learned
by personal contact, and there was no great variety of this
kind of music. I recall "Money Musk," "Old Zip Coon,"
"Old Dan Tucker," "The Sailor's Hornpipe," "Arkansas
Traveler," "The Irish Washwoman," and "Turkey in the
Straw."

All told, we had lots of music, such as it was; and by and
large, I guess the type of music performed and the skill of
the performers were about on a par with the musical appreciation of the audience.

*The Big Blizzard of 1888—an account limited to our own
personal experiences only*

As I said at the start, this book is not a history, but about
things, events, and people that have played some part in my
life, so all I will tell about this famous and vicious storm
are the experiences of our own family. For details about it,
you can consult your encyclopedia.*

The dates of this storm were January 11 to 13, 1888. So
far as we could judge, based on what we were told later,
the first indications that a storm was brewing showed up in
Rushville between nine and ten o'clock the morning of the
eleventh. My brother-in-law, Steve Auker, had gone to
town and he said that the early morning was clear and
lovely and warm. But very shortly a change came. A mist
began gathering and a sort of film spread over the sun. The
wind started to rise and in a few minutes swirls of dust and
fine particles of snow began chasing along the streets and
roads. At first there was so little snow that the disturbance
was mostly dust; but suddenly out of nowhere came the
snow, borne on a fierce northwestern wind. Then folks who
had seen one before knew that a big blizzard was in the
making; and immediately all concerned took steps to prepare against its as yet uncertain duration and ferocity.

Knowing that his family was at home with little means
of protection and very little fuel, Steve started back in his
one-horse cart shortly before noon. He got only as far as
Ed Skiles' farm, four miles east of Rushville, when he was
forced to give up and take shelter. For ten whole days
Steve's family had to get along as best they could, knowing
nothing of his fate nor he of theirs.

---

* There is an extensive literature devoted to the Blizzard of 1888.
A volume of eye-witness accounts has been compiled by W. H.
O'Gara (*In All Its Fury*, Lincoln: Union College Press, 1935).—*Edi-
tor's note*

There may have been worse storms than this one, but in 1888 there was virtually no snow-fighting equipment or means of communication. Day after day people were found in fence corners, ravines, and other places frozen stiff, and all the while no one able to help or even knowing where help was needed. All that could be done was just wait until the snow settled down enough to permit walking or driving on top of it, or until a friendly Chinook wind came along and wiped it out almost in a flash.

Among the many heroic incidents of the storm, one of the best-known was the epic of teen-age Minnie Freeman, the teacher at Midvale School near Ord, Nebraska. When the fuel was gone she tied her pupils together with a lariat and led them safely to shelter; but other teachers and pupils were not so fortunate. Because in many parts it struck just as children were leaving school for home, the blizzard was widely known as "the school children's storm."

On our farm, the approach of the storm made itself felt a little later than in Rushville; and being in the country we didn't have the chance to study its growth and development as could people in towns. It looked much like an ordinary storm except that the snow particles were much smaller, finer, and harder. Fortunately we figured we might as well prepare for the worst, and proceeded to do so. Plenty of oats straw was put in the stables for the horses and cattle, and a quantity of heavy bedding straw thrown in where the hogs could arrange it to their liking. Even though we felt sure we'd be warm in our well-built sod house no matter how cold it got, we piled up the wood for our heater and cookstove. And so, having done all we could for everything and everybody, we went early to bed.

The next morning we knew that we had been hit by a blizzard, and hit hard. We found our bedding covered with a soft, white powdery substance rather like talcum powder. The snow was so fine that it had actually sifted through between the layers of sod—and this in spite of the fact that the walls were almost three feet thick and had been settling down for nearly three years. Our first thought, of course, was to see what had happened outside, and when we tried opening the front door we discovered that the snow had piled up almost to the roof. But Mother's head soon started working. She poked up the fire in both the heater and the cookstove, and put on all the big pans we had, including her copper-bottom wash boiler. Then we all started digging out the snow and carrying it to this collection of vessels to be melted down, which made it much easier to dispose of. I don't know how many shovels of snow make a gallon of water, but before many hours all the receptacles we owned were filled with water, and there was a narrow runway cut which let us out of the house for several feet.

If you happen to have gone through a blizzard, you know that the snow will pile up behind a house or barn until it is almost buried, but out in the open where the wind gets a full sweep there may be a stretch where there is hardly any snow at all. After we left the shelter of our house, we ran into a clean-swept space that took us almost to the first of our two stables without any more heavy shoveling. After we had gotten in to see how the livestock was faring, we hauled all the warm snow water out to the cows and horses and got some swill to the hogs and feed to the chickens. Then, so far as our immediate family was concerned, we could sit back and say, "Let it storm." We knew nothing about Steve being lost somewhere between Rushville and his home, and with our livestock doing well, cows giving milk as usual, hens laying on schedule, all we had to do was await the decision of Mother Nature as to when she would start clearing things up.

The next day we got to the well, and by the end of the three-day blizzard we were in fine shape to take care of our stock. Many others did not fare so well; but that's life.

After all, we said to each other, this was a new country and folks had to learn how to look after themselves. . . . Yet in spite of the prevalence of this rather cold-blooded attitude, many heroic and noble things were done in time of prairie fire, epidemics, or trouble of any sort. Folks were inclined to talk tough, but soon broke down into heart-warming sympathy when the occasion called for it.

Illustrating this, here is an incident which had nothing to do with the blizzard, but does show how emergencies could bring people together even when they were at outs with each other.

The year 1888 had been the best of all our life on the farm in Sheridan County. Every crop we had planted turned out most bountifully, and both humans and animals had plenty to eat. Our horses were especially happy, for oats yielded over a hundred bushels to the acre. So you could say that we were all feeling our oats and, having done so well, we decided to attend the County Fair at Gordon to take a look-see at what other farmers had raised.

On the morning of our trip we were up and ready to go just a little after sunrise. That year we could take a whole wagonload in and since a prize was being offered for the largest group in one wagon, we added the McBride girls and a few others to our own family, which at that time consisted of Mother, Ira, Minnie, George, and myself. Of course we had put together a lot of good eats for the trip: fried chicken, homemade bread, tomatoes, pie, etc. This was stowed aboard, then off we drove, eager to see our very first fair, and the horses seemingly as agog as we were. Brother Ira was driving with Mother beside him on the front seat, the only easy riding place in the wagon. The rest of us were crammed in the wagon box, sitting in every conceivable position, but what did a little discomfort matter when we were on our way to such a big event, the biggest so far in our lives.

We had made about half the distance to Gordon when our Polish neighbors, Albert Hindera and his family, tried to pass our wagon. We were in the road—what road there was—and Albert turned out on the grass to go around us. But Ira had a different idea. Under his breath he said, "No Polak is going to pass us," and gave the team their heads.

Neck and neck we raced on for quite a distance, and then Albert cut in ahead of us, forcing our team a bit off the road. At this point, one of our horses broke a tug (trace, or drawing strap) and the neckyoke slipped off the end of the wagon tongue which dropped and skidded along the surface of the ground for some hundred feet. Then it struck a soft spot and dug in. Our wagon was catapulted into the air and landed upside down, scattering its occupants all over the landscape.

When the dust settled, there was Mother clear across the wire fence of a farm, with the overturned wagon box on top of her, and the rest of us strewn around the adjacent terrain. Fortunately no one was seriously or even painfully injured, but our wonderful food was pretty much mashed up. Mother had a badly skinned shin and of course blamed Albert Hindera for it and for causing the accident. She did not scold Ira for his part in the upset—he was only defending the honor of the family and the prowess of his team.

After an interval to collect ourselves and fix up the harness and damaged wagon, we went on our way again. We were not very many hours late arriving at the fair, but all the female members of our group developed what was the prerogative of every woman in those days, a sick headache. This spoiled the day for them and we started back home quite early in the afternoon. When we reached our farm, we found that the cattle had broken through the gate at the upper end of the chute and were crowded around the water tank, fighting to get at water which wasn't there.

The tank was bone dry because lack of wind had kept the windmill idle all day.

The pay-off of this dismal excursion was that a feud built up between Mother and Albert, and for almost a whole year they snubbed each other completely. Then one morning about three there came a tapping on our bedroom window and the voice of our neighbor saying, "Please, Mrs. O'Kieffe, come quick, Anna is going to give a baby." Mother bounced right up and in minutes was at the bedside of Albert's Anna. At six A.M. she was back to report that Anna had a fine, big baby boy, and that was the end of the feud between Mother and Albert Hindera. For the rest of our stay on the farm we were all the very best of friends and neighbors.

My most inglorious Fourth

Speaking of our disastrous trip to the Fair brings to mind another occasion I was all set for fun but instead wound up a social failure. But first it will be necessary to set the scene and tell you a bit about the fellow whom I omitted from my account of Sheridan County Fauna—*Mephitis mephitis*, known to some folks as the pole cat and to most of us as just plain skunk, but it doesn't matter what you call him for no name could make him sweeter.

While our farm was almost as level as the top of a billiard table, to the west of us there was a short range of hills, the crown of which was filled with a sort of undeveloped rock we called native lime. (This was what we used to plaster our house.) There was nothing in the way of timber, not even a shrub larger than a tumbleweed, but the growth of bunch grass on these hills did provide some shelter for wild fowl and small animals. Among the latter was that lively little black-and-white creature with the cute bushy tail that he usually carried jauntily over his back. He was like a lot of people in this world, nice to look at and perfectly harmless under most circumstances, but a critter that anyone could easily get along without when he was in a bad mood.

In the early summer of 1888, almost nightly we experienced the loss of at least one and sometimes several of our most precious hens—the hens on whose daily production we depended so much for the few things we could afford to buy at the Rushville stores. Because their death always followed the same pattern—throats cut, blood sucked away, and no other marks of violence—we concluded that a skunk was doing the dirty work. Strengthening our belief was the fact that a hole burrowed under the slatted gate shutting off the lower half of the henhouse door was not big enough to let in a larger animal. And as the clincher, there was always that somewhat musky odor which is typical of a skunk when he is in good humor. So, the night before the Fourth of July we set a spring trap in this hole.

Early on the morning of the Fourth our assorted family noses told us that we had either caught a skunk or something that had married into the skunk family. (Talk about your modern deodorant that lasts all day, here was an odorant that lasted all night and was still going strong.) It was now up to my brother George to dispose of our captive, and he did this very effectively with his 12-gauge shotgun. But the flavor lingered on, wafted from a distance of less than seventy-five feet to the spot where we were trying to eat our morning meal.

Being assigned to get rid of the animal's carcass, I took the trap, its chain, and the corpse way out in the oat field several hundred feet from the house, and buried the whole kit and caboodle deep down in the rich Nebraska soil. But still there was that odor, and it semed to become more pungent and sickening as the hours wore on. However, we had done all we could, and there was nothing else to do but stand it.

We finished the rest of our morning chores and shortly before noon I put on the best and only good clothes I owned, and started out to join the young folk of the neighborhood in a Fourth of July picnic at Wasmund's home some distance southeast of our farm. There was a funny sort of bump in the ground between our two places—hardly a hill but still high enough to hide our two houses from each other. For this reason, none of the folks gathered there could see me coming until I had topped the crest of the rise. But the wind must have been just right because the gang knew someone was coming all right—they didn't know who, but they were sorry the welcome mat was out.

Entirely ignorant of these advance impressions, I came jauntily over the hill expecting as usual something like "Strike up the band, here comes Charley." Instead people shot away from me in every direction—and not even distance could lend enchantment, for the odor from the skunk's distribution system seems to grow stronger when you're far enough away so it can come at you from all sides.

No one wanted to play, and all the picnickers lost their appetite, so finally in sadness and sorrow I wended my outcast way back home where things could hardly be any worse and my own family was conditioned to me. Thus was spent the most memorable Fourth of July of my life—and though I was just one day short of being nine years old, the memory is still so vivid that at times I think I can smell it.

Hunting and fishing for results as well as sport

Picture a country where there was plenty of game, but little ammunition and practically no money to buy it—that was the situation which prevented us from living in a sportsman's paradise. My older brothers and the Wasmund boys managed to get their hands on some shells now and then; but when they did every shot had to count. Consequently, a good deal of maneuvering had to be practiced which might have been frowned on in circles where sport is just that—sport—and has no vital connection with either the family diet or pocketbook.

For instance, in hunting geese—the fowl that was the most common during the fall and spring seasons—these young nimrods resorted to the very unsportsmanlike plan of stalking the birds. First, a gentle bossy cow was walked to the place where the geese usually sat down, where a planted field bordered on grass. Maybe they would find some geese already there; but if not, they took it easy and waited their arrival. The cow meanwhile was happy to eat the grass— time meant nothing to her. After the game birds had showed up and were busy picking up grain and other tidbits, the boy behind the cow would nudge her gently and start her moving slowly toward the flock of geese. When the gander showed signs of restlessness but before he sounded his warning call to the flock, the hunter would step out and shoot at the sitting birds. The idea was to get geese for food, not to set up things to give them a sporting chance.

There was one slight drawback to this method. After the first shot had thundered out not too far from old bossy's sensitive ears, she became gun-shy; and thereafter on seeing the hunter rise up from his hiding place the uncooperative animal would bolt. This usually resulted in no-contest between the boys and the geese for that particular day. A new cow would have to be chosen, and it became a question of which would run out first—the geese or the supply of cows which had not yet been under fire. Since the Wasmund family had more cows, the Wasmund boys got more geese.

Jack rabbits were plentiful all year round, but they had to be shot one at a time and their food value hardly justified the cost of an expensive shotgun shell. So eventually the boys developed a less expensive and more effective method of handling Jack. In the early fall, after the corn had been cut and the shocks removed from the field, they would rig up two farm wagons and put a half-dozen hunters in each. The wagons would be stationed about three hundred feet apart and a strand of barbed wire stretched between them. When the wagons proceeded across the field this would drift backward into a loop. As it skipped along, any rabbit hiding in the zone would jump up and head out of there— which was the signal for one of the boys in the nearest wagon to let fly. Usually there would be more than one rabbit scared out, and at times you could get two with a single shot.

As an interested spectator, I have seen the two wagons bring in fifty or more rabbits in one evening. After being divided up by the hunters, the jacks would be taken home, skinned and gutted, and then hung head-down on the windmill tower to freeze and cure until wanted for cooking and eating. The four legs and maybe a bit of the breast was all that was edible or desirable.

Ira got a grouse now and then; but we seldom enjoyed that delicacy. Ira was our most productive hunter. He loaded his own shotgun shells and in his equipment kit had a wad cutter, a capping device, a bullet mold, and such other items as he needed to be quite self-sufficient. I have watched him many times as he cut wads out of the leg of an old felt boot, and they seemed as efficient as the wads you could buy in stores. Where he got the money to buy powder and so on, I never knew.

Fishing, as far as I was concerned, was mostly done in Rush Creek, three miles to the south of our home. At first I walked down, but later on I got to take our pony Maude. She would be hitched to my small cart, and I stowed a little lunch in the cabinet under the seat. My pole would be the first willow I could find that was long enough and straight enough to permit me to stand on the creek bank and cast out far enough to reach the spot where I thought a fish might be. There were plenty of bullheads and a shiny silver species that I think might have been perch; and there were also sunfish but of a smaller size than I have since caught in the lakes of Minnesota. But they were all fish and while I never got very many, I enjoyed making the effort. This was especially true when the crops were all dried up and there was not a thing for me to do on the farm, even if I had wanted to.

My bait was usually some poor helpless grasshopper that I could catch easily. I never used a frog or minnow, but at times tried a bit of salt pork sneaked out of the kitchen when Mother wasn't looking. On arriving at the creek, I would unhitch and unharness Maude and give her a nice place to graze where there was much finer grass than at home. There she would stay on her lariat until I wanted to move so far away that transportation was desirable.

One day I had been luckier than usual and had a nice string of pretty good-looking fish anchored to the soft creek bank—a long willow withe was poked through the gill of each fish and held on by a crotch at the lower end. After a rather long trip up the creek, I went to get my day's catch and start home. But when I pulled up my willow, there was nothing on it but some fishy remains. The explanation—and the villain—was swimming nearby in the form of a huge mud turtle. This guy made me so mad that I jumped right in after him and by a bit of clever juggling managed to toss him out on the bank. With vengeance in my heart, I tied one of his hind legs with Maude's lariat and fastened the other end to the axle, and proceeded to drag Mr. Turtle through the sand and dust of the road all the way home. This was hardly the sporting thing to do, but he had ravaged my catch of fish and he had to suffer.

When I got him home, I threw him in the stock tank and there he lived for several weeks. Then one day the cattle broke through and drank the tank dry, so I transferred my enemy to the swill barrel and left him there to fatten for another few weeks. What additional punishment I had in store for him would be hard for me to say at this late date, but whatever it was it never came to pass. When the cold days of autumn came, my anger also had cooled off, and I took him out and turned him loose.

Beljacks: the true story of why I do not have the first quarter I ever made

The turtle could hardly be counted as a pet—he was a prisoner of war—and I doubt if my Belgian hares could be classed as pets either. For one thing, I didn't have them in my possession long enough to work up much of an acquaintance, and in any case I hadn't acquired them to serve as pets but as a commercial investment.

An advertisement urging the reader to RAISE BELGIAN HARES FOR FOOD AND PROFIT had somehow come to the attention of our Bohemian neighbor, Anton Thiel. Like many another, he bit, only to find out the hard way that there was no market for his studs and does at the big profit the advertisement promised. In fact, it seemed that everybody he approached was already in the Belgian-hare game and swarming with unsalable merchandise. The result was that the Thiel family ate Belgian hares seven days a week.

I came into the picture when I went over to Anton's place to help with the threshing. Perhaps I had better explain that all such work was trade-work: you worked so many days for your neighbor who, in turn, did the same for you. A man with a team counted as the equivalent of three days' work by a man without a team; but there were complications. For example, a farmer who owned a real first-class team of horses would absolutely refuse to put that team on the horse-power that ran the threshing machine. If you have ever seen the contraption known as "the horse-power"—and if you like good horseflesh—you will understand why. Watching today's wonderful threshing outfits sail through a grain field in nothing flat, it is hard to appreciate the way things were done seventy years ago. Everything depended on horse-and-man-power, with little brain-power involved.

The horse-power machine consisted of a central set of gears with five sweeps, or poles, sticking out like spokes of a wheel. A team of horses was hitched to each sweep, with the team's lead straps tied to the sweep ahead of it. The driver was seated on a box above the central mechanism, and when he cracked his whip the five teams were supposed to start moving counterclockwise. "Supposed" is the operative word. As the circular movement began—quite a short turn for any really decent horse—some animal was sure to object to the tug that rubbed his hind leg. Soon he would have kicked over the traces, and the entire operation would be snarled up.

With a bad-acting horse or so removed, and by patient and slow starts, the steady movement of the horse-drawn power unit was established. The gears under the driver's seat engaged the tumbling rod, which sloped down to the ground in order to permit the horses to step over it; thence it ran by a series of knuckle joints over to the separator some twenty-five feet away, and then sloped upward to engage the gears that rotated the cylinder in the mouth of the separator itself. Here was where the actual threshing of the grain began and here was the post of the cock-of-the-walk, the feeder. His job was to rake off the bundles from each side of his platform and feed them into the mouth of the machine in such a manner that the cylinder teeth could grab them just right and shake the grain from the straw. From here on it was a routine operation carried on by the different parts of the machine.

Since a boy would hardly be allowed to do any of the "scientific" work around the set, I drew the straw pile—the hardest, dirtiest, sweatiest job on the lot. Modern workers protected with goggles, masks, gloves, and insect-repellents can have little idea what I went through that viciously hot September afternoon. What wouldn't I have given just for a pair of those cheap canvas gloves that were later to be available at any store for a quarter! Out in our western country the hollow stems of all grains draw up quite a lot of alkali dust by capillary attraction; and this combined with a goodly amount of smut in both wheat and oats, plus swarms of buffalo gnats, was what I had to stand while handling the straw pile.

I smeared my face with axle grease to protect against the stinging gnats, but I could only put it on up to the underside of my eyelids, which became my Achilles' heel. Even though my mouth and nose also soon were stopped up with alkali dust and smut, I had to carry on. If the straw-carrier should clog because I hadn't kept the straw cleared away and properly stacked, the big black devil who was feeding the machine might make good on his threat to spear me with a pitchfork.

Well, all things come to an end, even bad things, and after

working from seven until noon we were called off for dinner. As many an old-timer will recall, this was supposed to be the real treat for the threshing crew. Most farmers' wives went all out to feed the men so well that they would mention the meal in glowing terms at the next farm on their threshing schedule. But either Mrs. Thiel did not care to compete in the culinary sweepstakes or else her man Anton dictated the menu. We had Belgian hare stewed in vinegar, boiled potatoes, cabbage slaw, and water.

Thirty minutes were allowed for this "bunny-break," and then we went at it again. The sun was hotter, the straw dirtier, and by now my stack was the highest thing on the place. Since buffalo gnats always hit for the highest object, I was "it" for the rest of the day.

When we finally finished the job about dark, we were rewarded with a dainty snack of cold Belgian hare. Then we were off to our homes for the night. Being the lone man without a team for the power or bundle wagons, I was the only one to be paid off; and Anton asked which I would prefer—twenty-five cents in cash or four of his Belgian hares to start me on the road to wealth. For some reason the latter idea appealed, and I took the rabbits.

Anton hunted up an old gunny sack into which he put the hares. Ignorant as I was in these matters, I could not tell whether he was giving me two "sets" or four of a kind. Anyway, I lugged my squirming booty home and, after some thought, decided to keep them overnight in the oat bin in our granary. Its board partitions were six feet high and tightly fitted. Into this safe-looking repository I dumped my future fortune and then, dog-tired, went to bed.

Bright and early in the morning I was out there to see if perhaps there already had been a harvest. Far from it. All I found in the oat bin was three piles of rabbit skin and a few left-over guts. It was clear that our old cat had done his work well, but I had put in *four* Belgian hares and there were only *three* corpses. How come? Well, as I learned the next spring, the odd rabbit had done what everybody had said was impossible. He had climbed up and over that six-foot board partition and fled to the cornfield. How do I know? With my own eyes I saw concrete evidence that the escapee had taken to wife—or husband: your guess is as good as mine—a jack rabbit, said evidence being what they produced in the way of an offspring. It had the body of a Belgian hare and the speed and agility of a jack.

I often wonder what became of these half-breeds. Perhaps I should have followed the matter up and gone on to fame and fortune as the proprietor of a huge ranch of hybrid "Beljacks."

As a postscript I might add that, generally speaking, jack rabbits seem to have had the Indian sign on the O'Kieffe clan. A few months after we had settled down on our property it developed that Mother would be permitted to take what was called a pre-emption, thus adding an additional quarter-section. Still later she was allowed to file on a tree claim: that is, the Government bet 160 acres of land that we couldn't get ten acres of trees to grow on it in ten years' time. For several years we laboriously planted our quota of young saplings, and in the fall and winter the jack rabbits no less diligently ate them off the ground. Although the Government eventually gave Mother a clear title for having made a game effort in the field of forestry, the rabbits and nobody else were the real winners.

If it had been my destiny to be a go-getter ranch proprietor (though not of "Beljacks"), I had a pretty good model to follow in the career of the Modisett brothers. [Albert R. Modisett settled in Sheridan County in 1885, and was joined the next year by his brother A. M. (Mayre) Modisett, their mother, and their sister Rosa. "When Albert Modisett took over the homestead, he had a team of mules, a lumber wagon, plow, tents, and food. In 1934 he ran 2,900 Hereford steers winter and summer. . . ." The site of the original holding on Deer Creek was about twenty-two miles from Rushville, at the center of the sixty sections the Modisetts finally owned. In the early 1900's Mayre sold out to Albert. The 1935 sale after the death of Albert was "probably the largest single-unit land sale to be made in Nebraska in the last quarter century or more."] * Before these enterprising, hustling young men came to Sheridan County from West Virginia, a flock of settlers, including us O'Kieffes, took up homesteads in the black-soil sections; and by the time the Modisetts arrived there was no land left excepting in the sandhills lying south of the Niobrara.**

The Modisett brothers were located on Deer Creek, a tributary of the Niobrara from the south. They started right out by doing something which was new to us: in making their filings they took up land four forties long instead of square as the other homesteaders had done. This gave these smart young brothers complete control of the upper part of Deer Creek, and as no one then had any use for the sandhills lying on each side, the result was that they wound up with a real ranch property although actually owning only their own original homesteads. This maneuver really paid off later.

We and many other homesteaders, being farmers and interested in milk-producing cattle only, had adopted the

* Sheridan County *Star*, special issues of May 9, 1940, and June 1, 1944.—*Editor's note*
** The author is mistaken. According to Mari Sandoz: "Old Jules located settlers on the table within ten miles of Rushville as late as 1892-3. Hundreds of settlers took up land on the hard table north of the river as late as the 1890's, and my grandmother took up a homestead north of the river, hard land, fifteen miles from Rushville in 1897. The Modisetts wanted a large block of range that no one claimed for range at the time, not owned, but claimed. That meant they had to get south beyond the line riders of the Newman and the Hunter ranches."—*Editor's note*

plan of knocking our bull calves on the head with a hammer
to dispose of them before they were old enough to take any
valuable milk from their mothers or from our precious supply. Thus we saved milk for butter and built up our she-
stock by saving the heifers only, which in time became
milk-producing cows. Learning of this bull-killing policy,
the Modisetts distributed to us and many of our neighbors
penny postcards on which we were to note the birth of
bull calves and then mail them to the Modisett ranch. In
return they would come and haul away the unwanted little
bulls and give us a big round silver dollar per head. Since
money was mighty scarce in that new country, we all
thought this was a fine idea.

Well, the idea worked with reverse-English. In the dry
years our good black soil disappointed us and we made no
particular headway farming, while at the same time the
Modisett boys were becoming the cattle kings of our section. In fact, before I left that country for good they had
shipped an entire trainload of cattle at one time to South
Omaha. Which goes to show that good new ideas worked
out with energy and enthusiasm can carry you a lot farther
than the stolid acceptance of things as they are, even though
it may be combined with back-breaking toil. This may seem
obvious, but Nebraska farmers and ranchers, many of
them, have shown themselves slow to accept innovations.
There is a lesson for them in the career of the Modisett
brothers.

The passing of Prince and Jack

Near the start of this book you met Prince, the fine Hambletonian horse we brought with us from Johnson County
and who was to be our driving horse as soon as we could

buy that nice buggy to which to hitch him. Well, we never got that buggy or the fine, shiny harness for Prince; and the only way he could serve us was, now and then, to be fitted with an old discarded harness and made to pull one section of the harrow when we needed to drag a plot of ground too small to justify using the three-section harrow and regular team.

As the months and years went by, old Prince spent more and more of his time grazing on the open field of grass just north of our cultivated fields and outside the cow pasture. When he had eaten his fill of grass, he would amble back to the house and take his place in the stable. But one day Mother noticed that he couldn't see very well, and before long she had to tell us that Prince was going blind.

From that time on we watched him with sadness as he slowly picked his way down the road from his pasture spot, sort of feeling his way along the packed part of the road with sensitive hooves much as a blind man would do with a cane. The road then was still just a pair of hardened ruts with grass or weeds on each side and in the center, but at the point where many rigs had made the turn-off to our house there was quite a wide space of hard surface, and this helped Prince to find his way home.

A day came when Prince could not go out any more. In the language of the local folk, he "got down"—that is, he was unable to get up on his feet. For a week or so we fed him as he lay on the ground back of the stable, but he grew so weak that Mother knew his end was near. One night at supper she said, "George, you will have to kill old Prince in the morning."

She might just as well have told him that he had been sentenced to the Pen for ten years for stealing sheep. But George was big for his age and very strong, so the next morning he went to do this heartbreaking job. On his way he picked up the heavy axe at the woodpile, and when he passed the granary he took a lusty swing at the corner post to get rid of some of his feelings. Unless the granary has been torn down, you will find there the deep dent made by the hardest blow George ever struck.

In a while he came back to the house, looking relieved. "Maw," he said, "Prince was already dead."

"I know it, George," Mother said. (I write it down "Mother," but in all my life I never heard her called anything but Maw.) "I knew how you felt about Prince, so about five this morning I fixed him up a nice pan of warm bran mash and put in a tiny pinch of strychnine."

So passed a real personality to us, a part of our family for many years. Now there was nothing left to do but drag his carcass over to the hills west of our home for the coyotes to feast on.

As for old Jack, he also was getting along in years, but he still enjoyed a good fight. In the summer he spent a lot of time in a nice cool pit he had dug for himself on the north side of our house, where the sun never struck. Like a spider waiting for a fly, there Jack would repose snoozing until someone drove in the yard with a strange dog. He never looked to see, but he could smell pretty well. There wouldn't be a move out of him until the visitor and his dog started to leave. Then Jack would come streaking out to pounce on the stranger, and unless they were separated promptly there would be one less dog to disturb him. Although he had lost most of his teeth, if Jack once got his jaws clamped on an adversary's throat it meant curtains in jig time.

He was the undisputed champ until the day that George Fisher, whose sister Lucinda had married brother Grant, drove in our yard to ask if there was anything he could bring us from Rushville. Now he had a dog that was some dog—a mastiff almost as big as a Shetland pony. Jack could not tell anything about the size of this newcomer just by his smell, so when the Fisher wagon started moving away, out he jumped as usual to launch his attack. Don't ask me how it was done, but that big dog literally picked our Jack up and swung him around over his head—somewhat like so-called wrestlers do on television—and then bashed him down *wham* on the hard ground of the driveway. That was that. Jack retired to his cool spot behind the house, and stayed there most of the rest of his life. He was beaten and broken in mind and body.

Late in the fall of 1889 we had an unseasonably hot day. There wasn't a breath of air, so the windmill wasn't running and the watertank was almost empty. To make matters worse, the cows broke through the pasture gate and came trooping down the lane to get a drink. Finding the tank low, they began to fight over what water there was, and a young heifer got hooked over the wall into the tank. When she went floundering around and splashing, Jack, hearing the excitement, came rushing from his lair as fast as his creaky bones would carry him. Among the innocent bystanders a neighbor boy, Eddie Wasmund, was nearest, and Jack started breaking up the riot by taking a bite out of Eddie's calf. Since he had almost no biting teeth left, the wound was not a deep one, and after Mother had dressed it that ended the fuss—or at least we boys thought so.

The next day brother George and sister Minnie and I went over to the tree claim to husk corn planted on the ten acres originally planned for trees. Arriving home with our wagon box well filled with snapped corn, George shelled off a handful of kernels and threw them at Jack, who was seemingly asleep near the granary in the warm evening sun. But Jack did not move, so George came back to take a closer look at him. Then he came running into the house, very excited.

When he announced that Jack was dead, Mother was ready with her usual definite reply. "I was afraid he might bite someone else, so this noon when you were all away I took a nice warm soda biscuit, opened it up, and put plenty of butter on the inside. Then I added a pinch of strychnine. Jack enjoyed his last meal very much. He didn't seem to suffer any great pain—just a little twitch and he was gone."

Thus once again Mother had faced up to what had to be done and had gone ahead and done it with as little fuss and sadness as possible. Here, as with Prince, she showed that side of her nature that was both practical and sympathetic, doing what was best for the animal and making things as easy as possible for the children. I don't think anything could be more revealing and more of a tribute to the character of a woman who never had much reason to live, never made any real progress toward achieving the kind of life she hoped for, never received much love or consideration from her own family. Quick to end the suffering of a dumb brute, she had to spend the last seven years of her life flat on her back, both hips broken, but never once considered an easy way out such as she had helped Prince and Jack to find. Instead, she smiled courageously through those years, lived as a benediction to all who served her, and went to her rest with unbounded faith that now all would be well for her.

I realize this is getting ahead of my story, but it is the best way I know to show what kind of a woman my mother was. My older sister Belle was another good example of the indomitable, self-sacrificing kind of woman who stood up well in the face of adversity and hardship, always being able to make do and always believing that a way would be found, and playing just as big a part as any man in the settling and development of our western country.

Belle and Steve Auker had been married four years when they came out to Sheridan County in 1886. By that time all the good farm land had been homesteaded, so they had to file on a tract just beyond the black-soil belt in the fringes of the Sandhills. There Steve built a dugout in the side of the solidest sandhill he could find, and supported the walls and roof with pine slabs which his neighbors helped him get. This was where Steve and Belle lived and some of their nine children were born.

Their great problem was water, which for some months had to be hauled from the neighbors' wells. Then one day Steve noted that willows were growing in a low spot between the hills on his land, and he knew that when willows grow, water must be near. He got a few feet of two-inch pipe with a sand point on one end and drove it into the ground in what seemed to him a likely spot. After letting things rest a day or so, he attached an old-fashioned kitchen pump to the upper end of the pipe, and lo and behold! he got water. Not too much, but enough for household purposes. It was "piped" into the dugout by means of the children. In my mind's eye I can still see the little tykes sliding down the hill of loose white sand just as if it were a snow-slide, only instead of a toboggan they used the cover of an old wash boiler. They would be clutching the proverbial lard buckets which they filled at the pump, then would trudge back up the hill to the dugout with the water.

Steve had neither health, strength, nor education, but he did have my sister Belle to serve as encouragement when everything seemed to go wrong. Once he tried to sell apple trees to the new farmers on the land west of where he lived; but the jack rabbits soon forced him to give up that idea. Next, he got a little supply of butcher knives and tried to peddle them, but with money so scarce every family that had any sort of butcher knife would make it do as long as possible—keep on grinding the blade down till there was nothing left except a splinter of steel. (This worn-out kind of knife was called a "toad stabber"—which is about all it could accomplish.)

One day when Steve had driven in to Rushville to pick

up a few items of food, he happened to drop in on Joe Thomas, the banker. In a small town like Rushville everybody knew everybody, so Joe welcomed Steve and they had quite a visit. As he was about to leave, Joe said, "Steve, why don't you go down in the south Sandhills, buy enough cattle for a carload, ship them to South Omaha, and make yourself some money?" Steve raised the perfectly logical question of what he would use for money, and Joe said he would give him a checkbook and Steve could pay for what cattle he bought by check. When these checks came in to be cashed at the bank, Joe would start figuring the interest on the money actually used.

This idea appealed strongly to Steve and he went home with a new glint in his eye and new hope in his heart. Two days later he was ready to start on his first cattle-buying trip. Because of his chronic ailment called Bloody Flux,* he had to tie two sheep pelts to the seat of his pony cart for cushions. Then he packed a few provisions and set out on what was to prove the greatest trip of his life. Later on I talked to the rancher where Steve made his first stop for the night, and he told me the sheepskin seat cushions were completely saturated with blood. But Steve kept on going and each successful day made him stronger physically, mentally, and spiritually. He bought his carload of cattle, shipped them to South Omaha, and cleared $284.00. From that day on, you could not see Steve Auker for the dust his activities stirred up.

He went up in the Belle Fourche section of South Dakota where they had been burned out by lack of rain and bought eight carloads of cattle, some of which he shipped east and the rest turned loose at home. By now, many of the early settlers had given up, especially those who had tried to make a go of it on the submarginal land to

---

* Probably dysentery.—*Editor's note*

the south and east of Steve's homestead. Because of this situation the County Commissioners passed a ruling that anyone paying three years of delinquent taxes would be given a deed to the property in question; and they fixed the tax rate at $13.00 per quarter section of land. Soon Steve owned the entire space between his home and the Niobrara River, with fences and gates set in where the main flow of travel went through. By buying and selling and keeping the old or unsalable stock at home, he soon had a fine big ranch well stocked. He built a very nice house on his original homestead, and had water pumped in from the new well with its powerful windmill, so my sister actually had running water in her kitchen—something that few, if any, other farm women in the country could boast.

Steve's success can be in part attributed to some timely advice and encouragement at just the right moment to spark his latent native ability, but much more to the undying confidence, patience, and selfless devotion of a really and truly good wife.

The O'Kieffe Boys: a kid-brother's-eye view

Since I am on the subject of my family, and before I go on to the next part of my story, it might be a good idea to take a look at my brothers while we are all still more or less together—or at least in the same neck of the woods. Mother and Minnie were to stay on the homestead until 1895, but the others had gone on their separate ways at various times long before then.

Although there was less than two years difference in our ages, brother George was always bigger, bolder, and much stronger than I. He was not mean to me in any marked manner, but never let me lose sight of the fact that I was his kid brother and that this made it necessary for me to conform to his ideas of behavior. Unless he slipped in a day or so while I wasn't looking, George never attended any school, although somehow or other he learned how to read and write. He never went hunting or fishing, never played any games with us, never sang or performed on any musical instrument, but he was always busy at something he felt was worth while. The only vice he took on while in our home was that of chewing tobacco, and he became quite proficient at it—for him to eat a whole plug in one week wasn't uncommon.

If there could be such a type in a crude family like ours, brother Ira (nine years older than I) might have been put down as the Beau Brummell of the O'Kieffes. He never attended school in our home district although he may have gone to one before we came West. At any rate, he had picked up a type of culture and refinement that put him way out of our class at that time. He could perform quite well on the violin, and had several guns and knew how to use them. My memory does not permit me to say just when Ira left home, but he must have been pretty well grown and perfectly able to take care of himself. One day we got a letter from him with some pictures. He had settled in Sheridan, Wyoming—then about the toughest town in the West—and was working in the local brickyard days, and playing for dances at night.

Ab, two years older than Ira, was my clog-dancing, mouth-organ-playing brother, and judged by the standards of the time and place he was pretty good at both. He could take an ordinary fifty-cent mouth organ, fit it into the top of a slightly flattened empty quart tomato can, and proceed to make music that—as the ads say of a certain cigarette—both pleased and satisfied. And when he cut loose with one of his special clog dances, he sure set everybody's feet a-tappin'. Aside from his ready wit and ability as a mimic, this was just about the extent of Ab's repertoire.

In our community and the others around it the mental average was such that it was quite easy to play jokes, provide amusement of a sort, start fights, and occasionally get someone killed. Because brother Ab's talent ran toward the lighter fun side, and because of his tendency to lord it over us younger boys with his superior savvy and quick-on-the-trigger comebacks, the following incident has always given me much satisfaction.

After we settlers had been given permission to cut pine trees for firewood from the timber strip forty miles north, the older boys had a program of making three trips for wood each fall. Supplemented by cow chips and corncobs, this would give us enough fuel to last all winter and carry us through summer as well.

On these trips the travel plan called for getting started at four A.M.; the wagon being empty and the horses fresh, the destination would be reached by noon. The rest of that day and part of the next would be put in cutting down and trimming trees; then the boys would load up and start for home. On the wagon, with its reach fully extended, would be piled three huge pitch pine logs, two between the standards and one in the notch between the two lower logs. The limbs that had been cut off these huge trunks were piled and tied all over the place, wherever the boys could find an inch of room. Altogether it made a goodly supply, both of small wood for a quick fire for cooking and of resin-filled heavy chunks to stoke the big horizontal heater which kept the place warm through long winter nights. Traveling with this heavy load was much slower, so the boys had to camp out the second night, and would arrive home around two in the afternoon of the third day.

In the fall of 1890, when it came time for one of their wood-gathering trips, George and Ab decided that I was old enough to go along, and I did, very gladly. We got started about at the usual time, with George and Ab occupying a spring seat that they had cleverly mounted on the front bolster of the wagon, now stripped to the running gears. I was cozily located in a big pile of hay for the horses, which was anchored to the rear bolster and covered with blankets. This was especially satisfactory to me during the first few hours as I was hardly awake when the trip began, and welcomed the chance to doze a little longer.

A few miles north of the village of Clinton we ran into the chophills marking the approach to the hillier timbered section; and near what they called a cut—a natural opening between the hills—there loomed up the first cavalcade of Indians I had thus far seen. To pass through the cut the wagons had dropped into single file, so we came into contact with the first one only, but my sharp little eyes took in the entire picture pretty well. We had stopped at an angle and I could see the tipi poles sticking out from under the rear of several wagons. Some of these poles were carrying an assortment of tin cans and buckets, pots, and cooking paraphernalia. Running around and under the wagons was a motley pack of dogs of every size and breed, and partially hidden by the body of the Indian driving the head wagon I glimpsed squaws and papooses galore.

Because the narrow opening of the cut was blocked by the Indians' lead wagon, we naturally had to stop; and here is where brother Ab stepped into the picture. Climbing down off his perch on our wagon, he held up his hand palm outward, and called out, "*How kolah*," this being the general word of salutation. The old buck responded with a grunt and put on a stony stare.

To one side of the lead wagon was just about the prettiest pony I had ever seen—probably weighing around 700 pounds, seal brown with four perfectly balanced white feet. (I figured out later that this graceful creature must have been sired by at least a Hambletonian, with a dam of pretty good blood. She sure was a beauty.) Pointing to this fine bit of horseflesh, Ab unlimbered his very best Oglala Sioux —largely, I suspect, for the edification of George and myself.

"*Shung-kah-kah leelah washtay*," he said, which can be interpreted as "Horse very good" or "That's a fine horse you have there." The next part of his harangue was part English and part bad grammar: "Swap. Me swap." And for a final installment he added the query: "*Muzis-kah tonah?*" (*Muzis-kah* = money; *tonah* = how much?) None of his display of linguistic skill had any effect on the Indian, so Ab hitched up his trousers, took a deep breath, and played the whole record over: "*Shung-kah-kah leelah washtay*, swap, me swap, *muzis-kah tonah?*"

This outburst of conversation left the Indian looking more than ever like his wooden counterpart that once stood out in front of tobacco stores. But Ab was determined to show us he did have a good command of the Sioux language, and doggedly repeated the mixture as before: "*Shung-kah-kah leelah washtay*, swap, me swap, *muzis-kah tonah?*"

Then at last the old buck opened his mouth. "You can buy him for sixty-five dollars." He waited a moment while Ab stood there speechless, then clucked to his team. The cavalcade moved on and we proceeded to our destination to cut down, trim up, and load our supply of firewood. Brother Ab, who did not have sixty-five cents, let alone sixty-five dollars, said nothing in either English or Sioux the rest of the way.

As Grant was thirteen years older, I knew very little about his early boyhood and teen-age life—whether he attended school or not, and what he did as he was growing up. For all practical purposes my memory of him begins

when we came out to Sheridan County and found him on
his homestead adjoining Mother's. During the interval between the time he and Mother had filed and she had returned to Johnson County to get the rest of us, Grant had
managed to break up some land, and on it had raised potatoes and squaw corn and a nice lot of turnips, rutabagas,
squash, and pumpkins. But he decided he was not cut out
for agricultural activity. There were four things Grant had
learned to do well: sharpen plow lays, weld broken parts
on farm machinery, shrink wagon tires to fit the wheels,
and shoe horses; so he built a simple little shop near his sod
house and opened a blacksmith shop. On November 14,
1888, he married Lucinda Fisher, whose family lived about
five miles to the southeast across the Niobrara, and in due
course Grant and Lu—as we all called her—were blessed
with two fine daughters, Ina Mae and Ethel.

Although there was little actual cash in the community,
Grant managed to gather in enough to keep going. This
money plus an occasional trade-in helped him to purchase
the needed supplies for his shop and to add a new item of
equipment now and then. In 1889, when the whole section
showed signs of total collapse, he moved to Rushville and
opened up a shop there. He did quite well as he now had
the entire area around the town from which to draw trade.

But fate had a new chapter in store for Grant: one day
out of a clear sky he was notified that he had been the successful bidder for the mail route between Rushville and
Pine Ridge, South Dakota. It was pretty close to thirty
miles each way, and the schedule called for a round trip
six days of the week.

In preparation for operating his Pine Ridge Stage Line,
my brother had built a very good barn on his property in
Rushville, and in the late fall of 1890 he sent for me to
move in with his family and take care of the fourteen head

of horses he had acquired. No doubt this was the turning point of my life. At any rate, it took me into a new kind of environment and gave me an outlook I had never had before.

IV

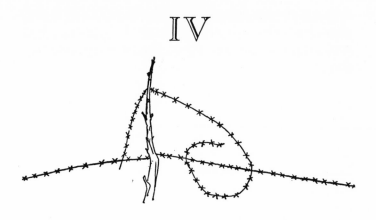

RUSHVILLE

Working for Grant in town

GRANT'S HOME, a nice one for the times, was located on a half-acre of ground at the eastern edge of Rushville. A fence divided it from the big barn, which was set on the north half of the lot, and the well and its equipment were on the south side of the fence so the family could get water without having to enter the barnyard. East of the big barn was a large area where the horses got exercise and fresh air when it was their time off.

Just north of Grant's was the home of Old Man Cunningham and his wife, and alongside his property ran the main road from the east. It ran due west for about six hundred feet past Cunningham's, then angled off northwest for a couple of blocks—or what would have been blocks if the town had been laid out that far—and then straightened out and continued westward. At the end of the angling strip was the big water tower and tank from which came all the water Rushville needed, as most folks had their own wells. West of the water tower you passed the Methodist Church and then came the biggest commercial building in town, a two-story brick-front structure that housed the governmental machinery of both Sheridan County and the village of Rushville. The top floor of this long building was used as an opera house where dances, shows, and entertainments were held from time to time. From here on was "downtown" Rushville, and after I went to work for Grant I was to see plenty of it.

For a lad brought up on the farm with its multiplicity of chores, there did not seem very much for me to do on my new job. I merely had to meet the stage as Grant drove it into the barn runway, unhitch the four snow-clad (or mud-covered) horses, unharness them, and put each in his proper stall. Next I filled the mangers with hay, put the right amount of oats in each feed-box, and then rubbed down the animals with wisps of dry hay, being especially careful to get all the icicles or frozen mud off their fetlocks. Since Grant usually arrived around six each evening, there was nothing more for me to do until the next morning.

Grant always harnessed his horses himself in the morning, although I did help him hitch up if he was trying out a new and frisky animal. I began the day by drawing water from the well—by far the hardest of all my chores. I turned a crank that rotated a drum around which the rope was wound, and this brought up a full bucket from the bottom of the 75-foot well. It wasn't particularly hard physical work, but at best it was chilly and at worst real bone-killing cold. Then, too, there was always the chance that the brake —used to slow down the empty descending bucket—might become slick from wear or from being ice-coated. When this happened, no matter how hard I might bear down on the brake lever, the bucket kept picking up speed on its downward way and occasionally things got clear out of hand. The bucket would crash to the bottom, unreel all the surplus rope from the windlass, and tear the stapled end of the rope from its moorings, pulling everything down into the well. Then there was nothing to do but get out the grab-hook and fish around until the entire mess had been recovered and everything made operative once more.

Later on Grant installed a windmill, which helped some, but it too had some bugs that caused trouble from time to time. It was the invention of Old Man Stephenson, a broom-maker when he could grow or buy the broom corn. Thinking that he saw possibilities in this contraption, Grant bought the first one as a demonstration model. Most every farmer already had a good well, but many of them lacked a pump and windmill. As the Stephenson automatic windmill would get a farmer all the water he wanted without the expense of putting in a pump and a hundred feet or so of expensive pipe, Grant figured he had a real salable item.

To begin with, the wheel up on the tower responded to the wind which was nearly always blowing in that flat country. The motion of the wheel activated a set of gears on top of the tower which rotated a drum, much like the one I had been using in drawing water by hand. As the drum turned it wound up the rope, pulling up the long bucket to the proper spot for emptying. At this point the gears were temporarily released, allowing the bucket to stand still long enough for a trigger to reach out and poke a valve in the bucket bottom. This permitted the water to flow out through a snoutlike elbow into a chute that carried it to the horse trough. During this outpouring period the wheel was still running, and after a certain number of revolutions the operating gears were once more engaged and the empty bucket sent on its way down for another load. However, on real windy days the wheel on top the tower traveled the operation up there faster than the emptying process took place down below, with the result that everything got all balled up.

Eventually Grant was forced to conclude that Old Man Stephenson's invention was a flop. He put in a pump and installed a real windmill—an Aeromotor, which I believe is still being sold—and from then on there was little trouble about water, save now and then during an unusually calm spell when we had to pump by hand.

An Indian scare and two Wild West shows: (1) Mrs. Asay and Buffalo Bill and (2) the show that went on the road

To the east of Grant's place was a rise of ground that was probably the highest point in the town. It was almost like a huge ball that had been sunk in the earth, leaving only the upper half showing. On this hill was the biggest and in many ways most attractive house in Rushville. Its real importance, however, lies in its tenants—then and later. In the fall of 1890 the man living in that fine home was Professor Wilson I. Austin, the head of Rushville School. But my first contact with him was not in the school: it took place the night of the Indian uprising under Big Foot and his Ghost Dancers.*

On the night of December 29, 1890, the usually suspicious white folks expected the Indians to attack the Holy Rosary Mission some thirty miles away, with the object of taking their children from the school. The only telegraph wire between Rushville and Pine Ridge Agency had been cut, so our home-town folk could only guess at what was going on up there, and how soon the fury of the redskins would be vented on us. A hastily organized Home

* Notes on the ghost-dance mania and the massacre at Wounded Knee begin on page 212.—*Editor's note*

[108]

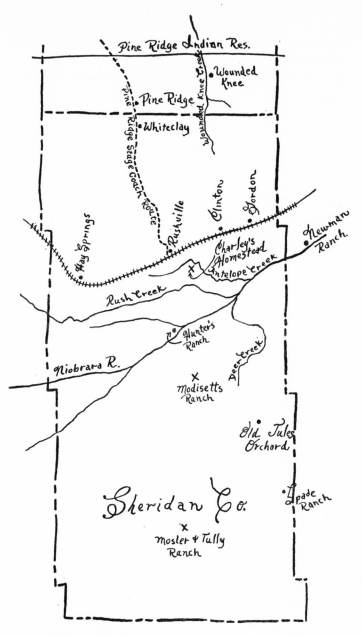

In this sketch map of Sheridan County, the scale is approximately fifteen miles to the inch.

Guard was thrown around the town, and every so often Professor Austin would drop in to hear if we had gotten any word from brother Grant who, of course, had not come home.

About all I recall personally of that night were the periodic checks of Professor Austin with his reports that all was well so far as the Home Guards could see. Being badly scared, I was mighty glad when Lu, Grant's wife, invited me to crawl in bed with her. In the end, none of the threatened perils ever materialized and the guards were disbanded. Austin was replaced by another professor * and new tenants moved into the hilltop house.

The newcomers were Mr. and Mrs. Jim Asay, and I never did learn where they came from. Along with them they brought their lovely but harum-scarum daughter Hattie and a son whom they called Ejie. Although somewhat of a dreamer or poet at heart, he was "antsy"—always on the go, never stayed in school for any length of time at one stretch, would take off and return when he got good and ready. This was the family that was soon to be entertaining a most unusual guest, none other than Colonel William F. Cody.

Because of my living in the Asay front yard (or their living in our back yard, depending on which way you were driving past), it was quite easy for me to get acquainted with Colonel Cody, at least by sight. Many a time I saw him in the yard with Mrs. Asay, or sitting on the porch with Mrs. Asay, or out driving with Mrs. Asay. It was always Mrs. Asay, never her old man.

She was the owner of a magnificent chestnut-colored gelding and a carriage different from any I had ever seen.

---

* Professor Austin was still on the job in the fall of 1891. According to the Rushville *Standard*, October 9, 1891: "The school bell now has a fire alarm attachment which was recently arranged for by Professor Austin."—*Editor's note*

[110]

It's easier to describe that rig than to name it. There was no top, and the seat was set up high to show off the occupants. The body was arched so that the front wheel could pass under it when a sharp turn was made. When the lovely lady herself climbed into the front seat wearing a large picture hat and long gauntlet gloves, and Buffalo Bill was royally seated by her side, the result was a vision of dashing loveliness and class. It was a sight that Rushville got treated to many times over the years.

In those days Buffalo Bill's hair was a deep rich brown, which he wore long, falling down to his shoulders. His Vandyke beard was also brown and always neatly trimmed. In fact, his whole appearance was that of a man in excellent health and there was nothing about him to suggest that he craved the limelight and public acclaim. As for Mrs. Asay, in her visible life at least, she was a lady of culture and refinement, always neatly dressed, always completely poised and at ease, and in business matters keen and astute. Her husband was just the opposite in about every respect—nearly always partly, if not entirely, soused (though sober enough to be ambulatory) and always very talkative. This meant that Mrs. Asay alone entertained Buffalo Bill on his various trips to Rushville, and she did so with all the niceties then available.

The usual morning drive of the couple was from the house down to the store, which Jim Asay—who already had gone down on foot—had open for business. One thing you could say about Jim, he was faithful, not a bit jealous of his beautiful wife and her association with Buffalo Bill.

In addition to the social side of their relationship, there was a business arrangement whereby Buffalo Bill or his business manager gave each of the hundred Indians chosen to travel with his Wild West Show a due bill for $40.00 on the Asay store. These due bills had to be traded out exclusively at Asay's within a period of two days from their

issue—which occurred on the day before the Indians' departure for the East. You can imagine the jam in that store as
Indian bucks, squaws, and papooses swarmed in, buying
goods of every description and smoking the free Sweet
Caporal cigarettes the Asays provided in a huge pan on
each counter. For the store it was the biggest two days of
the year.

Several days before the date of their departure the Indians who had been chosen to perform in the show began
to arrive in Rushville, along with their friends and relatives.
By the day before they were scheduled to leave, the Indian
campground just across the tracks was filled with tipis and
overflowing well beyond its usual limits. The streets of the
town, especially Main Street, became a scene of unusual activity, with the mixed population milling around, visiting
the stores and buying all sorts of things. (I remember one
enterprising housewife had learned that homemade pies
were a favorite delicacy of any Indian who had a single
dime to spend.) Of course the members of the immediate
families of the show troupe had their precious forty-dollar
due bill to blow. If they had been given this amount in cash
they would have been scattered all over Rushville, but it
was good only at Jim Asay's and there it would be used up
fast.

We youngsters got our biggest kick when, a little after
noon of the last day, a hundred or so Oglala Sioux assembled in the middle of the dirt street and performed their
colorful and exciting dances in full regalia—war paint, war
bonnets, breechclouts, anklets of little jingling bells, long
strips of leather on which were sewn pocket mirrors picking up and reflecting glints of sunlight. You may have seen
Indian dances at national parks, rodeos, and other western
celebrations, but this one in Rushville was the pure quill.
These Indians were not paid to perform—they wanted to
do it, and there was spirit and fire in every movement they

made. When a weirdly painted savage swung his tomahawk at you in the course of his gyrations, you almost felt that he meant it and you'd better play safe and dodge.

After the bucks had done a few numbers there was the squaw dance in which the wives and sisters of the favored ones took part. It is hard to describe this dance, but if you will wrap a plain black or blue army blanket around your shoulders, letting it fall like a skirt to within a few inches of the ground; and if you will decorate the blanket with beads, all sorts of shells, and silver coins punched and sewn on; and finally, tie a flat sort of belt around your waist, put moccasins on your feet, and stick a few brightly colored porcupine quills in your hair, then you will be all set to do the squaw dance, Gay Nineties version.

The dance itself was the acme of simplicity. Each squaw kept her feet close together and sort of bounced up and down without appearing to move. I doubt if anyone's feet got over two inches off the ground, and no one moved more than a few inches to right and left. It was all done in perfect rhythm accompanied by the tom-tom beat of the same drums the bucks had used. What was fascinating about this dance was the total lack of emotion or muscular activity. With expressionless faces, the squaws went through their performance impassively, almost like puppets on strings.

After the dancing came the speechmaking, usually by Chief Wounded Knee. His talk was always to the same effect—that it was the desire of the Great White Father in Washington (*Wahk-pominy-tipi*) that each Oglala Sioux behave himself as a good Indian should, thus reflecting credit on his tribe and the nation he represented. An interpreter told us what Wounded Knee had said, like his modern counterpart giving it to us in short jerky chunks, each chunk being preceded by "Wounded Knee he say—"

At the end of the party, and before any of the departing

Indians could stray off and get involved in something, they were all marched down to the depot at the end of Main Street where two passenger coaches were waiting. They were locked in these, and there they stayed until the Omaha-bound passenger train came through at midnight, picked up the coaches, and whisked the Buffalo Bill Indians away to start their new life. Perhaps "whisked" might be considered a bit strong by modern standards, but the train at times did hit thirty miles an hour.

Now let's skip over several months and have a look at the homecoming of these same Indians who, in the intervening period, had toured the country and maybe even traveled abroad with Buffalo Bill and his aggregation of fast-riding, straight-shooting, stunt-performing cowboys, stage coaches, and trick horses.

When the day of their return to Rushville came around, we all assembled in the small house that Harlan and Lulu Johnston * had rented for the school year. Train Number 29, as I recall, was due in from Omaha at 1:08 A.M., and the only way to find out if it was on time was to send someone to the depot a half-mile away to ask the night telegraph operator. Our party had quite a bit of fun during the forepart of the evening, but shortly before midnight we sort of drooped on learning the train was two hours late. However, we were there for a purpose, so we made a batch of pancakes and ate heartily. Right now I do not recall what we drank: there were no bottled soft drinks then and I doubt very much if young people had as yet acquired the coffee habit. After eating, we spread blankets on the floor and all

---

* Harlan and Lulu Johnston, whose parents lived in the country—I believe down toward the Niobrara River—played little part in my life excepting for the one term I shared their little shack in Rushville. The most startling thing Harlan ever told me was that his dad was a nephew of General Johnston, the well-known Rebel leader. Harlan's dad fought with the Union Army, and Harlan told me his father had remarked on the number of times he took a pot shot at his uncle.—*Author's note*

laid down side by side like so much cordwood. Of course we were fully dressed and the girls of that day were so well protected from neck to ankle that no one even thought of doing anything except catching a few winks of sleep.

After another trip to the depot we found that the train would be in around five A.M. and eventually it did arrive. Here were the Indians whom we had last seen in war paint and feathers now clad in Prince Albert coats, Stetson hats, patent leather shoes, and all the accoutrements of the well-dressed man of the period. Where they had left us filled with good advice, now they were full of bad whiskey or lemon extract or hair oil or anything under the sun that contained even a little alcohol; and where they had gone away with all they owned on their backs or in their hands, now they were returning with more useless junk than they could carry—two baggage cars full. I never got a good clear look inside, but no doubt the cars contained notions, fancy ties and loud neckerchiefs, gaudy trinkets, lots of perfume, and everything drinkable that an Indian could pick up, legally or otherwise.

It was far from a pretty sight to see these noble red men literally roll out of the coach door and into the arms of their respective squaws to be dragged over to their tipis, there to spend the next few days sobering up. Who was to blame? Well, all I know for sure is that it wasn't the Indian who started making whiskey and selling it to the white man —and for me that's a good enough indication of where the blame belongs.

The wonderful Pine Ridge Stage Coach, and my first experience "in the money"

It soon became evident that what Grant earned in Government pay was not enough even to buy the needed oats and hay for his horses, but the Indian uprising proved a timely development so far as his personal financial situation was concerned. In came the soldiers and up went the volume of passenger business to be hauled at a profit; and in addition there was extra pay for favors performed by Grant for the army officers and the tradesmen at Pine Ridge Agency and in Rushville. Business was actually booming.

During most of his stage-driving career, Brother Grant used an ordinary hack with removable seats and button-down side curtains—it was in this rig that he had hauled away many of the officials and important folk during the Indian uprising. But finally he succumbed to the romantic and bought a real honest-to-goodness stage coach. He had to go all the way up to Fort Randall to get this prize and he drove it back to Rushville for its maiden trip on the Pine Ridge Stage Line.

This rig was just like the ones you see in movies and on TV shows. It was a rock-away model with an all-leather body on wooden framework cradled on powerful leather springs. Up front where the driver sat there was a large boot, with room enough for at least two besides the driver. Inside, there were two seats facing each other, each easily seating three people. At the rear there was another, much larger boot for luggage or freight—or even people, should the need arise. Altogether it was a mighty imposing rig and attracted a lot of attention when Grant drove it in. Most of the Rushville folks had seen many sorts of covered wagons, but hardly any had ever seen a real stage coach—one that was now to operate out of their own home town.

Grant put his new rig on the regular daily run to Pine Ridge and back, and used it until he gave up his mail contract, which must have been about 1892. (I know he stayed in Rushville long enough after the Indian trouble ended to buy several condemned cavalry horses, and to turn down the outright gift of some 30,000 bushels of oats that the army did not care to move away.) No doubt the old coach wound up working in the movies, as outfits like that one never really wear out. Who knows?—I may have watched my brother's rig in some Wild West film during my later years.

I expect many rode in the coach just for the novelty, but as all Grant's passengers were unloaded downtown before he drove up and turned the outfit over to me, I had no chance to see who had been aboard on any particular day. At times I heard him mention such personalities as Captain Penney, Major Brookes, "Indian Jim" Finley,* and Bob Pugh who was the issue clerk at Pine Ridge. I doubt if he ever hauled any of the big military brass as they usually had their own conveyances and official escorts. Since conversation builds up ideas that later pass for actual facts, it wouldn't be safe for me to name any more people—in fact, I'm not sure that General Miles was even at Pine Ridge during this short-lived uprising. [He was.—*Editor's note*] Grant also had quite a bit of contact with Buffalo Bill, and one year helped him choose the Indians for that season's show.

---

* Captain Penney was the Administrative Officer at Pine Ridge after the uprising had been put down. Major Brookes was second in command during the actual fighting. Only thing I heard about him was from the regular soldiers when they camped across the tracks in Rushville, and to whom I sold the *Saturday Blade* or *Pennsylvania Grit* and from whom I picked up empty whiskey bottles. They spoke of Major Brookes in a sarcastic manner as being the "Old Maid." Indian Jim Finley had the trading post concession at Pine Ridge and it was for him Grant did most of his favors while he was driving the stage.—*Author's note*

[117]

The last year that Grant ran the stage was a pretty good period for him. He had made so many friends during and after the uprising that lots of good things kept coming his way, whether deserved or not. This together with the far-too-frequent gifts of whiskey kept him in a fine humor most of the time.

On the morning of the Fourth of July, 1891, Grant seemed to be in a more mellow mood than usual, which is not the common morning-after experience, but anyway I was to be the beneficiary. In those days all the money was silver—the Indians had no use for paper money and neither did most of the white folks, for their mode of living made it infeasible to carry or keep currency. So most of the cash that Grant brought down to Rushville from such men as Indian Jim Finley was in silver. As a rule I never had a chance to see this money, but on the Fourth of July the banks weren't open, hence Grant was keeping Indian Jim's money at the house over the holiday.

After breakfast Grant said, "Kid, how would you like to celebrate today? How would you like to run up to Hay Springs where they're going to have a big time?" When I told him I had nothing saved up for such a trip, he went to the corner of their bedroom, rolled out a nail keg, took off the lid, and said, "Help yourself."

There right in front of me was more money than I even knew existed. The keg was full to the very top with shiny silver dollars. In case you have never seen a nail keg (and I guess they are less common than dollars now), I should tell you that all the nails in hardware stores then came in large wooden kegs big enough to hold about fifty pounds. Just how many silver dollars were in that keg I had no idea —and I was in no mood to count them out.

Acting on Grant's urging, I picked out two big round dollars—the most money I had ever gotten my hands on in my life. No amount of money I have received or handled since has loomed as large. Down to the depot I walked, on air every step of the way. I was dressed in a $9.85 suit that Aunt Lu had purchased for me the year before—the first "boughten" suit I had ever owned. At the depot I paid fifty-nine cents for a round-trip ticket to Hay Springs.

When I got there, I went at once to the celebration grounds and tried to enter into the festivities, which already had started. Naturally I bought some firecrackers first and shot a few of them off, putting the rest in my pocket. But before very long some wag dropped a live piece of punk in that pocket and off popped the firecrackers, completely ruining that side of my wonderful suit. Then I bought something to drink, and some candy and cake, and eventually I found my bank roll had dwindled down to three little pennies. Like a good sport (which I was not), I bought three huge sugar cookies, ate a couple of them, and—in a most devil-may-care manner—sailed the last one off in the air the way small boys used to sail flat stones or tin can lids.

By this time I had picked up the usual sick headache, so I walked down to the depot where I curled up on one of the hard wooden benches and awaited the train that would take me back to Rushville and normalcy. I have celebrated high, wide, and handsome in many ways and in many places since then; but never have I started with such high hopes and ended with such a headache.

My last view of Grant and his real stage coach left a most vivid impression on me. He had given up his stage job and was very busy working as an inspector for the Deering & McCormick harvesters. However, he allowed himself to be talked into taking the Rushville baseball team to Hay Springs for a very special game. Here is the way they left town: Up in the driver's boot with Grant were three players; inside on the double seat were eight; and in the rear boot were five more. The bats, balls, and uniforms were piled on top of the coach.

Before embarking, Grant had taken a swig or two in Charley Evans's saloon and was therefore in tiptop condition to give the players the ride of their life. And they got it. I can see them yet as the coach swung around the curve just beyond Savage's pond and then onto the main road headed west. Grant had hooked up four of his saltiest horses for this final fling, and as I got my last glimpse of the show through the gathering dust the men in the rear boot seemed to be practically floating out behind on the thin Nebraska air. Under Grant's inspired piloting, the rig was traveling at such a clip that the boys were blown off their perch; they literally clung on by their fingernails until my brother slowed up and let them drift back again into their seats.

If any of the players are still alive, they probably have forgotten how the game came out, but I doubt if a one of them has forgotten his last drive with Grant O'Kieffe.

How to teach the Metric System

Aunt Lu, Grant's wife, decided that I had done so well working for them that I deserved an education; and in the spring of 1893 I made my first entry into Rushville School, Intermediate Grade, under Miss Patience Tulle. The next year I stayed on the farm and went to District 38 again, but later returned to Rushville.

The Rushville school building was a square boxlike structure containing four rooms. In the lower right-hand corner as you came in from the north was the Primary Room; when a child was all done in there he moved to the east and became an Intermediate. In due time he would move upstairs, right over the room he'd been in, and become a Junior. Finally, he moved to the west room as a Senior. From there, he just had to move outdoors because there was no place else for him to go.

During the years of my off-and-on experience in Rushville School, I did manage to get one full year in the Junior Room under Miss Glenn, and it was in the middle period of my Junior Room life that the incident I'm going to tell took place. Miss Glenn was entirely new to me—not only because it was my first year with her, but because I had never seen such a lady before. She was well educated, refined, and gentle, but she was also athletic—a combination as novel to me as it was to most of the local population. In a woman out there, muscles were a sign of hard farm work and not the result of calisthenics, lawn tennis, rowing, or other forms of ladylike athletics practiced in the effete East. Miss Glenn was an Easterner—that is, she had come out to Sheridan County from Tarkio, Missouri.

There was the usual assortment of pupils in the Junior Room that year—some quiet and proficient, others rough and hard to discipline. But there was one who outclassed everybody in every detail of conduct and cleanliness—Harry, the son of a local butcher who ran his butcher shop just the way Harry ran his life—sort of catch-as-catch-can. There were no pure food laws in those days and no ordinances on sanitation, so the good folks of the community either held their noses while in the butcher shop, or never went in. Well, like father, like son: Harry was slovenly in dress, uncouth in speech, and decidedly unclean bodily. On the day in question he had on a turtleneck sweater that looked as though it had been "turtlenecking" Harry for many, many months. There was an almost tangible residue from unwashed sweat that the collar had rubbed off Harry's body. No one wanted to sit next to him because of his appearance as well as his unpredictable behavior.

We happened to be studying the Metric System in our

arithmetic class, and Harry was asked by Miss Glenn to recite one of the tables that dealt with the liter. He started
out in his usual gangster-type fashion and pronounced the
word "litter." Miss Glenn corrected him, but Harry
brushed this off with the reply, "Liter or litter, it's all the
same to me."

Miss Glenn's irritation showed on her usually calm and
dignified face. "Harry," she said, "the word is 'liter,' and
that is the way you will please pronounce it."

"You call it your way, and I'll call it mine," was Harry's
comeback. " 'Litter' for me; 'liter' for you."

This was too much for Miss Glenn, and she leaped on
Harry like a jungle tigress. Grabbing him by that loose-fit-
ting, dirty sweater collar, she swung him around off his
feet and whammed him against the cast-iron leg of my desk
so hard that it broke. Then she picked Harry off the floor,
set him upright, and said in her gentle, well-modulated
voice, "What is the word, Harry?"

"It's liter, Miss Glenn," he said earnestly. "Liter."

Many years later I met this lovely and capable lady in
Minneapolis on the streetcar. We had just gotten nicely
started conversing about the early days in Rushville when
she had to get off. In all the excitement I forgot to get her
new name—she told me she had been married. So now I
don't know where I might find her: I would certainly like
to hear her views on how to handle today's juvenile delinquent.

I don't care what became of Harry.

I begin to learn about women

I have already mentioned Hattie Asay, who lived in the big
house on the hill, the only daughter of Mr. and Mrs. Jim

Asay. When I knew her, Hattie was by far the liveliest of all the young lassies in Rushville. She was active and alert, quick on her feet and quicker with her tongue, but only clean words came out of her mouth.

It was one of my greatest joys to walk with Hattie down the long plank sidewalk from the corner where we met to the school building a quarter of a mile away. Some days we would cut across and pick up Daisy Clybourne or Edith Thomas or Ethel Thompson—never any boys, so I had pretty much of a monopoly on Hattie for a couple of years at least.

We would talk about many things as we walked along: nothing very heavy because neither of us had seen much of the world as yet, although Hattie had seen some of Omaha when the Asays went through it on their way to settle down in Rushville. We went to simple parties now and then, and occasionally to an ice cream social at one of the churches, but our school never gave any entertainments.

Hattie was always well dressed, since her folks had the store. Some pretty classy fabrics could be obtained there, but not ready-made wear for women which wasn't then in vogue. Also, her father had to make a few trips to Omaha during the year, and he usually brought both Hattie and her mother something new and nice. She was quite tall and very graceful, wearing her clothes well and carrying herself most ladylike. If she were alive and young today, I'm sure she would be a mighty classy tennis player and a better than average golfer; and would put on a good show on a spirited horse. But tennis hadn't yet come to the West and we'd never heard of golf, so Hattie and I merely walked and talked.

It must have been rather an odd pair that Charley and Hattie made on their way to school. She wore the best while I wore what in those days was considered about the worst—tan or mouse-colored denim pants cut and sewed the best she knew how by Mother. The pants were cut high at the bottom to save cloth, so they were neither long pants nor knee pants—just halfway in between. This mouse-colored fabric had one very serious drawback: it turned a brilliant orange color where you had been careless and piddled a drop or two. It made things very embarrassing because one pair of pants had to last a long time, during the course of which they would naturally pick up a number of orange-colored spots and streaks. But Hattie and I did not mention such things. She never commented on my clothing or conduct, and most certainly I found nothing about her to criticize.

One day she gave me a sample of what folks in those rather narrow times would have called tomboyism. I was at the water bucket in the school hallway during recess, and was enjoying a refreshing drink from a huge dipperful of water. Then along came Hattie, with fun in her eyes. Naturally I had no idea as to her plans when she stopped abruptly in front of me. Raising her pretty, flouncy skirts clear up to her knees, she swung out a well-stockinged leg, and let fly with her foot. Result: the dipper and its contents went sailing through the air, some of the water falling on my head and shirt, the rest hitting the wall and ceiling. During that brief moment I learned more facts about the female figure than could possibly have been acquired decently in any other way. But to Hattie it was just an impulse, quickly obeyed and quickly forgotten. She wasn't trying to show me how she was put together, or how many fancy petticoats she was wearing, or how trim were her ankles and calves. She merely felt like dipper-kicking at that moment, so she kicked my dipper, and I was glad she kicked my dipper.

At our parties some of the kids played Post Office, but I always kibitzed. I was sure no one of real quality would want to kiss me as I never smelled any too fresh and certainly had no clothes that would attract anyone. So I never was chosen to receive any mail that would demand a kiss for it. But Hattie, she would have taken home a lot of money if there'd been a fee for each buss she got or gave away. No doubt those puritanical folk who watched her so sharply, perhaps enviously, listed Hattie as bound to end in the class called "bad women" by those who made up the groups known as "nice people."

A big contrast to Hattie was Stella, the stepdaughter of the man who bought out Gus Humboldt, our free-bologna-to-good-boys butcher. She was fussy, nervous, dainty in a sort of phony fashion, and always getting offended, or insulted, or hurt in some way, either in school or at parties. But where she really shone at picking up grievances was on our frequent skating parties.

We would find two horses of some kind and hitch them to a long, cumbersome bobsled, fill the wagon bed with straw, drive by the school and appropriate a good supply of firewood, then be on our way to Wallenstein's pond about four miles to the southwest. At the pond the wood was unloaded, some at each end so we would have light and warmth when a skate went on the blink or ankles got overtired. After the fires were lit we were ready for skating, many with really fine gliders on shoes or boots designed for skating, but I with only my well-worn shoes and a pair of old skates the like of which I've not seen for years.

You drilled a small hole in the heel of each shoe and screwed on a small plate around the hole; then you inserted a small dingus on the heel of your skate into this heel hole and turned your skate around until the front was at the toe of your shoe. Next, you unloosened the clamps with a clock key and put your foot in the skate; then after you tightened the clamps you were all set to go. But my shoe soles and heels were so worn that the leather quickly became water-soaked and soggy. No matter how tight I twisted the key on the clamps, they merely pushed in the soggy leather and the skate would drop off. In the end I became a fire-tender, much to the joy and comfort of the rest of the party.

On such trips Stella was always getting crowded by someone—usually a boy she didn't like, or insulted by some crude remark that jarred her assumed dignity, or getting her leg pinched by a stick of cordwood being shoved roughly against her by some careless passenger. Altogether, whether at school or at play, you could be sure that Stella would get mad or become hysterical, and we were all expecting it whenever she made part of any group. Even the teacher quite often had to allow her to go home because of the headaches brought on by some heinous offense committed by somebody.

The contrast between Hattie and Stella went deeper than anybody realized, as I found out some years later—1898, to be exact—after I had moved to Omaha. I was working in the Union National Bank and also drilled with the Nebraska National Guard—which nightly enacted the charge up San Juan Hill for the edification of audiences at the Trans-Mississippi and International Exposition. It was lots of fun, and I had a chance to see the show before and after the sham battles. One evening I happened to be on the Midway Plaisance when out of nowhere came Stella. She seemed glad to see me, but was probably in her usual mood of finding everyone wrong but herself. After some small talk, she said that she had a show on the Midway called "Girls of All Nations," and gave me a ticket to it. Of course I went, and I saw more of female nudity there in a short fifteen minutes than Hattie would have shown me in a week of dipper-kicking episodes. Stella's girls of all nations didn't do a strip tease—they had nothing much on to strip—but the visitors, who always act differently away than they seem to do at home, really ate the stuff up. I have not seen or heard from Stella since that night.

One day not long after, I was out collecting for the bank and had in my pouch several sight drafts on Kirchbraun and Sons, Produce Dealers. The drafts had bills of lading attached, and the firm had to pay the draft before they could get the bill of lading which would release the car. When I walked into the office, there in the cashier's room stood Hattie: she was bookkeeper and cashier. We were surprised and delighted to see each other, but since we both worked long hours during the week Hattie asked me to visit her on Sunday.

She lived in two small rooms on the third floor of an old building. It was a sweltering hot July afternoon, and the rooms were right up under the flat tin roof. I was hardly inside the door when Hattie proudly showed me her two small children, about which I had not been advised. She was earning $15.00 per week, out of which she paid $3.00 for a daytime baby tender. There was no ice, no fans, nothing to make life more comfortable in those two little rooms; but they were getting by somehow.

Hattie told me that she had married George Newman, the night operator at the Rushville depot. After two children had been born, George had gotten itchy feet and had headed out for parts unknown. In those days there was little or no effort made to retrieve delinquent husbands and of course alimony had not yet been invented. So Hattie and her babies had to make it alone, and I'll bet they did too.

Rushville Who's Who *

As a young fellow growing up in a small town, there were two things that interested me greatly: the jobs that were being done and the folks that were doing them. If Rushville had had a *Who's Who*, here are some of the people who would have been in it:

Sol Pitcher held forth at the U.S. Indian Supply Depot, and was responsible for every item that came through to be issued to the Pine Ridge Indians. Sol was not a Jew, but he had a nose on him that would have made "Schnozzola" Durante extremely jealous. So far as I know, Sol did his work very well and was completely honest at his end of the line.

Then there were Judge Patterson and Judge Westover, jurists of no small culture. Westover had a little the better of things because he had a fine family of children to carry on the name whereas Patterson was childless,** without anyone except his brother Billy. Billy added little if anything to the family standing, unless it be he who inspired that old saw: "Who hit Billy Patterson?"

A most dignified character with a very solid military presence was old Colonel West, who for a time ran one of the Rushville hotels. Once I worked for him for a few weeks as a sort of combination train-caller and bellhop.

One of the grandest of the older men was William Alexander, who owned the biggest and best store in town. I had the extreme pleasure of working here many Saturdays, counting out eggs and weighing butter. Two happy and memorable events took place during my time in his employ.

* Supplementary notes on some of the persons mentioned in this section appear on page 218.
** The author is in error. The Pattersons had three children.—*Editor's note*

There was the day I walked home for supper with his beautiful daughter Mary, and had the unusual experience of drinking out of real glassware, eating off real china plates with real silverware, and—for the first time in my life—using a linen table napkin. The other grand feeling came when I was given the trigger combination of the money till, and was actually allowed to make change and put the money received in the proper stalls in the tray.

Among the more ordinary folk who did things but on a less lofty plane, there was the village barber, John Bayne. He had remarkably fine, smooth, soft hands, and the boys all said he was a very clever poker player. Indeed, they had bestowed on him the monicker of "Old Brass Tacks" because, so they said, he could sit in a game until he had worn the brass heads off the upholstering tacks. Charley Edgell took over the barber shop when Old Brass Tacks finally gave up.

Speaking of poker brings to mind the name of Sam Sing, our Chinese laundryman. I was told that Sam was quite a proficient poker player and was always welcome to the sessions of that fraternity. He did all the work for some families, especially men's shirts, and the local sports all depended on him for their fancy and high-priced apparel. I saw Sam only in his laundry as he ironed shirts, with the end of his long pigtail firmly grasped in the hand that held the handle of the flatiron. He was a faithful attendant at the Methodist Church and could always be depended on for a ticket to their ice cream "sociables" and oyster suppers.

Then there were the Blacks, Frank and Bill, who claimed that in their livery stable they had the finest horses and classiest rigs west of Omaha. Frank was the gentleman of the two, and wooed and finally won Bertha, one of John Bayne's lovely daughters, both of whom he managed to raise to perfect womanhood despite the loss of their mother early in life. The other girl, Bessie, married Ira Avant, and they participated in the famous run for the land when the Cherokee Strip was opened in Oklahoma. Word came to us Rushville folks that they had gotten some choice land and that the town of Avant had been incorporated by them. All I know for sure is that today there is a fine little city in Oklahoma named Avant, and I hope it is the town Ira and Bessie started.

One of the men I most admired was old Gus Humboldt, the butcher. (Not Harry's father.) He could always be counted on for a nice, juicy, piping hot ring of bologna every Thursday when—just by mere chance—I came around. His stone smokehouse was in back of the shop and in there on long poles hung the many rings of bologna, each a work of art created by an old man who knew his job and loved it.

For a time the saloon was run by Charley Evans, and unless you have tried it you have no idea how much you can learn going into places where you're not, at your age, supposed to go. Charley Evans never once invited me into his saloon, but on several occasions he did invite me out. Between the ins and the outs I managed to see a lot and learn a lot about the other fellow and the way he would react to things around him.

It often happened that I'd be around there when the German band came to town for a short stand in Charley's saloon. There were always three members of the band, and always one had to be tall and skinny and one had to be built more like a meatball. The third bandsman could be almost any shape, and usually was. One played the piccolo and one the tuba, but for the life of me I cannot recall the third instrument this trio used. The three strolling players would march to the saloon with all valves open, thus attracting some of the outsiders who had not been planning on venturing into the so-called den of iniquity. Once inside, the German band would cut loose with polkas, schottisches, and dreamy waltzes, and between numbers they would quaff giant mugs of beer, their only recompense. They did not play for money, just beer, and I've always wondered how they could hold all that was given to them.

There was another music-maker whose activities were confined almost entirely to the saloon. From somewhere in the East came the swarthy, rather pudgy Italian harpist with his instrument on his back, carefully wrapped in black oilcloth to keep it dry. No doubt this man had camped with the rest of the tramps at their regular hangout under the railroad bridge just east of town; there was water there and a little shelter. The Italian's program was very simple: he'd walk into Charley Evans's saloon, find a seat, undrape his harp that stood almost seven feet tall, and just start playing. His stuff sounded good to me, and from the music I've heard since then I'm sure he played real classical numbers for those untrained but truly appreciative cowboys gathered in the town's one place of entertainment. After the silent old fellow had rendered a few selections, his hat was passed around and a few odd coins collected therein, mostly nickels and dimes as pennies were not in general circulation then. Once again the huge harp would be enshrouded in its sad-looking wrapper and onward would trudge our wandering minstrel who said very little, letting his harp speak for him.

Finally, Charley Evans sold his saloon to Tommie Dowd, who many people said was too good a man to be a saloonkeeper. George Evans, Charley's brother, had the finest jewelry store in those parts, and was married to the beautiful and gracious daughter of Lawyer Tom Redlon.

I must not forget the town marshal, Dave Gosh, for it was Dave who arrested me for the first and only time in my life. It happened that the snowballing was good one Saturday morning, and I and a few other lads were having fun along the south side of the Commercial Hotel. Dave watched us for awhile and then walked away, and for no reason at all I socked him in the back with a real squishy one. He wheeled and asked who'd done it, and being truthful always I owned up. Dave corralled me and took me to the sheriff's office, a block away. It turned out that Sheriff Essex had left town on a business trip, so I was turned over to Mrs. Essex who happened to be my Sunday School teacher that year. She promised the marshal she would take good care of me, and she did. I was given some cookies and a glass of milk and sent home.

Because I will speak of them later in connection with my life in Omaha, I will only briefly mention here Johnnie Jones, the lumberyard man, and Joe Thomas, the banker. He had the bank where Mother borrowed money to replace the goods we lost in the train wreck in 1884, and on which she paid two per cent a month for so many years.

Although he may not yet have done anything of great importance while I was around in the early '90's, the name of Jules Sandoz is probably now the best-known one of all. To most of us who so frequently saw him striding down the middle of Main Street, he presented a figure both pathetic and formidable. His dress and his conduct were his trade-mark: they made him distinctively "Old Jules." From his round fur cap, made of the skins of water animals he had caught himself, tanned by his own process, and cut and sewn in his own home, to the overshoes he wore always, regardless of season or weather, he always commanded your attention, though different people had widely different ideas about him. Since he never walked the street without his long barrel rifle ready for instant action, some saw him as a potential killer. To others he was only a freak who had allowed the new West to turn his head a bit too much toward the sensational. Most of us knew from local gossip why he wore overshoes in season and out—because of a terrible accident a few years before, which marked him for life with a painful limp.

What we did not know then, what we could not even imagine, was that Old Jules had a better education and much higher IQ than nine out of ten of those watching and pitying him. Hidden by his outlandish dress and behavior, his powerful brain and his poetic imagination were clicking away all the time. His later accomplishments brought this out clearly, and to a large degree served to confound his critics. Most of the bad things Old Jules had been charged with doing were undertaken in self-defense—against conditions and in circumstances forced upon him by his enemies or by crooked men in public office. And no matter what else may have been said or rumored about him, he was a truly patriotic citizen of his state and nation. His later years pretty well proved that.

Putting together what I knew then with what I have learned since, it seems fair and honest to cite Jules Sandoz as one of the truly important men of his era. He it was who first started people thinking along fruit-growing lines, and who built up the first real horticultural program in the Sandhills. Thanks to what he began against so many odds, there is today a better fruit-growing acreage in Northwestern Nebraska than in most sections of that state. He grafted horticulturally while far too many others were grafting politically. By their fruits shall ye know them, and the fruits of Jules Sandoz, the "Burbank of the Sandhills," are now known all over the nation.

*More about my homelife and education, including
an account of the graduation of the Class of 1896*

Entirely without intent to criticize and without resentment, I must say that my only contacts with culture or refinement came from outside my own family circle. The very first such contact that I can recall came from my instructor in the Intermediate Department at Rushville School, that sweet and most knowing teacher, Miss Tulle. Next came two of almost equal importance: Mrs. W. W. Wood, my Sunday School teacher in the Presbyterian Church, and our leading merchant and my first part-time employer, William Alexander.

It was some three years or so later, when I was sixteen or seventeen, that I went to live in the Sawyer household. Right now I cannot recall just how I came to meet the Sawyers and to be taken into their home, but somewhere along the line fate brought us together and for that I am most thankful. In their home I learned some big lessons about personal care and habits, and right conduct, not from any special effort at correction but just by virtue of the very atmosphere that surrounded me.

The Sawyer family originally lived in Iowa—near Boone, as I recall from Mr. Sawyer's telling the story of heroic Kate Shelley, famed for saving so many lives by crawling across a damaged railroad bridge and flagging down the train just in time. This had happened quite near the Sawyer's Iowa home, and Mr. Sawyer could recite all the details with great completeness and clarity.

When I became a member of their household, besides the parents—Mr. and Mrs. Clarence R. Sawyer: both quiet and unassuming, both educated and talented far beyond the average of that day and community—the family consisted of the son, Clarence Orson, and the two girls, Opal and Lucille, three as fine young folk as ever blessed any home anywhere. There was also Ponto the dog, and even today I never watch or listen to the Lone Ranger with his Tonto, without experiencing a sharp pang of memory that takes me back over sixty years.

My arrangement with the Sawyers was sort of cooperative. I moved in with them, becoming to all intents and purposes one of the family. Every week or so, Mother would drive in from our farm and bring a roll of butter and potatoes, cabbages, or eggs to help pay for my keep. While there was not a great deal of work to do, I did chop some wood and performed other farm chores as needed. C. Orson —called Ort by everybody, as I will do from now on—was the oldest in the family, but I must have been a little older than he as I was one class ahead of him in school, and I wasn't that much smarter. Ort carried his nickname well into his mature years when he became quite a personality in Nebraska agricultural affairs.

If any stranger had stopped by, I am sure he would not have been able to tell who was a member of the family and who wasn't in this clean, happy, Christian home—poor, but in every respect high grade. The Sawyer house was about two miles northeast of Rushville, and the four of us young people walked to school in town each morning and back again in the evening. If there was a social function in town after supper, we repeated the four-mile trip. There were no rigs to "thumb" in those days, and maybe once in a blue moon we'd catch a ride. We packed a family lunch box for the four of us and ate together at noon—in fact, we had everything in common except clothing. We boys could wear nothing of the girls', and when Ort and I were dressed each of us had on everything he owned, so there was nothing to exchange. We truly lived as one big happy family although Ort did some things I didn't exactly like, such as eating a big slab of bread and sugar in bed. (The principal thing I had against this was that I did not happen to care for bread and sugar at night; I preferred to sleep.)

In every way I respected and admired the Sawyers, and Ort and I having so many things in common could easily have gone into business together had we remained in touch. If fate had not taken me away from that section, I am sure that Opal and I could have married and made quite a success of it, although at the time I was living there our feelings for each other had not gotten past the proper brother-and-sister stage. But Opal did give me the wonderful lapel bouquet I wore the night I graduated.

With brothers George and Ab away on some uncertain working trip, and with me staying at the Sawyer home while taking my last stretch in the Rushville school, it seemed best that Mother and Minnie move to town. This they did, and lived for a few months in the home of brother Grant. When he and his family moved to Butte, Montana, this place was sold and we had to rent a small shack in the southwestern part of Rushville, not too far beyond Savage's pond. Grant's neat little home, with his huge barn, splendid well, and modern windmill brought the staggering sum of $125.00 for the whole works. Which goes to show that real estate value is created by just one thing: demand.

An incident which sticks in my mind occurred in March or April after we moved into our new home. During a heavy snowstorm in the latter part of winter somebody's shoat had wandered away, got lost, and frozen to death. When the warm spring sun had melted part of the snow, its frozen body was exposed to view. As the sight of a dead animal on the prairie was nothing new or unusual, we just let the dead hog lie where it had fallen.

One evening at sundown there was a rap on our back door, and on opening it I found myself confronting an old

Indian buck dressed in a lightweight canvas blanket that had once been white.

"Me good Indian," he said. "Me want *Koo-Koshya*" pointing to the dead hog some two hundred feet away. Like most Indians, he preferred to ask for what he wanted rather than to walk off with it and perhaps later be accused of stealing. Not to be outdone as a linguist, I said, *"Tch,"* the word of assent, and that ended our conversation and the transaction.

While the old fellow gathered in his prize, I stood watching. First, he took off his blanket and laid one edge of it close up to the hog's back; then, grasping its stiff legs, he flipped it over on the blanket, gathered up the four corners, threw the improvised sack over his shoulder, and marched off to his tipi. No doubt he and his family lived high off the hog for many days thereafter.

For five years of my school life, as I have related, I was obliged to alternate between our country school and the one at Rushville. This gave me a record of a few months in the Intermediate under Miss Tulle, a year in Junior under Miss Glenn, and most of two years in the Senior Room —corresponding to high school—under Professors Snodgrass and Frank Disney.

A year before we were slated to graduate there were nine in our class, but when May of 1896 rolled around we had dwindled down to two. Hardly worth having graduation exercises you might think, but we had them just the same, and here is the program given the night I got my diploma—the first member of the O'Kieffe family to do so.

Memory permits me to tell you that there were some pre-graduation activities, and on the night before the big day we did the town in style, driving the horse and buggy of O. F. Farman, the local druggist. The exercises were held in the Court House Hall, with a goodly crowd in attend-

COMMENCEMENT

—OF THE—

Public Schools,

Rushville, Neb.,

Friday, May 29, 1896, 8 O'Clock P. M.

FRANK T. DISNEY, - - - PRINCIPAL

GRADUATES, - $\begin{cases} \text{CHARLES O'KEIFFE.} \\ \text{CLARENCE MANN.} \end{cases}$

MUSIC,..Band
INVOCATION.
SOLO,..The Holy City,
LILLIAN ALEXANDER.
RECITATION,..The Loving Little Girl,
FLORENCE FARMAN.
ORATION,..The Campaign of '96,
CHARLES O'KEIFFE, '96.
RECITATION,..The Seventh Grade,
SUSIE ESSEX.
RECITATION,..Good Luck,
EARL CUNNINGHAM.
ESSAY,..Work Today,
ANNA WOOD.
RECITATION,..Simon Grub's Dream,
JOE WESTOVER.
MUSIC,..Cornet Duet,
MESSRS. MUSSER AND KINNEY.
ORATION,..American Heroes,
CLARENCE MANN, '96.
RECITATION,..Little Mischief,
JEANETTE GLENN.
RECITATION,..The Schooner Hesperus,
ELLA BROWN.
ESSAY,..Educating a Girl,
OPAL SAWYER.
MUSIC,..Band
RECITATION,..The Old Sergeant,
SARAH FREESE.
RECITATION,..The Particular Man,
BEATRICE WILSON.
ESSAY,..Hope,
TESSIE SHARP.
RECITATION,..The Little Black-eyed Rebel,
JOHN EDMUNDS.
SOLO,..Selection,
LILLIAN ALEXANDER.
Presentation of Diplomas by W. W. ALBERT, President of the
School Board.

ance. My oration was on William McKinley, the Republican presidential candidate. I was not at all nervous and everybody said I did well. My classmate Clarence Mann * also did his part well, and altogether our graduation could be called a complete success. Since Clarence died several years ago, I am the only remaining member of the Class of 1896—in fact, with a few possible exceptions, the only one present at the graduation exercises who is here today to tell the tale.

The Rushville Silver Cornet Band in which I played the B-flat cornet and which was led by John Musser, son of Old Man Musser the banker

The great majority of those who came out West to start a new life were just ordinary folks, but mixed up with them were a few with exceptional talent. It was from this group that the Rushville band was created. In our membership we had at least four cornet players who would be welcomed in almost any musical organization. Few of us realized what was in them until they came out to band practice and showed us what they could do.

John Musser, the oldest son of Old Man Musser who ran one of the Rushville banks,** started the band and was its leader while I lived out there. John was one of the four fine solo cornetists we boasted, and another was Frank Jen-

* My information is that Clarence later married Florence Barnes, the lovely daughter of our Rushville elevator and grain operator.—*Author's note*
** The Citizens Bank, organized by M. P. Musser & Company, was the third to be established in Rushville. It had been preceded by the Bank of Rushville, established by H. A. Chamberlain, and the Farmers and Merchants Bank, established by Joe Armstrong. The First National Bank, which the author refers to as "the Joe Thomas bank," was organized in 1889.—*Editor's note*

nings. The names of the others I have forgotten over the years. I also knew the other Musser boy, Logan, who had graduated the year before I did. Since how I came to meet him is a story with some rather interesting ramifications, I hope you will pardon my digressing from the band long enough to tell it.

During my Junior year, a young chap from back east had moved to Rushville and had brought with him the football idea. Association football, I believe he called his brand of the game. At any rate, it was played with a round ball which had to be ordered from back east. This took money, and I being as always fresh out of that commodity, Logan Musser loaned me my quarter to help buy the football. When it arrived, the team started practicing under the tutelage of Clyde Rosseter and eventually I paid back the quarter, which Logan saved. Later on, he bought a ranch with it and married Clyde's sister. Although Logan has passed away, the Fawn Lake Ranch remains one of the outstanding spreads in the central Sandhills.

Now back to the band, which I was invited to join by John Musser who also loaned me his old B-flat cornet. When John had us pretty well trained, he accepted an invitation for us to play at the McKinley rally at Chadron, Nebraska, in midsummer of 1896. On that whole trip we were treated in royal style—went to Chadron in a private coach hooked on to the evening train, and on our arrival were driven to the Blaine Hotel in a huge band wagon. We had a suite at the Blaine in which to clean up and store our instruments until time to play. Then we marched down to the dining room for the finest food I had thus far enjoyed in my life. When the torchlight parade began, we were given the place of honor and played for a nice long time, comfortably ensconced in the flossy band wagon. It was a wonderful success. Then back to the depot to await the coming of the train from the west which would take us home to Rushville.

Two weeks later we were asked to repeat the trip for the William Jennings Bryan rally. We had the same private coach for our train to ride to Chadron, but on our arrival —no band wagon. So we had to march about a half mile— not to the Blaine Hotel but to a tent where we were fed by the Ladies' Aid. When the parade started, still no band wagon—we were asked to march on foot like the ordinary torchlight bearers. During all this, John Musser had been getting madder by the minute. After we had played a few bars of a marching tune, he blew three toots on his horn, and we all fell out and walked down to the depot in utter disgust.

John summed up his feelings in a very few words—"Just like the damn Democrats." Not a very nice thing to say, but as well as being a musician he was a banker's son, and so no doubt a Republican.

It was in this summer of 1896 that I made the acquaintance of an invention which soon was to be of interest to all musically inclined people whether they played an instrument or just listened.

As I have previously stated, a young lad can learn a lot by horning in every chance he gets, and this was the precept I was acting on the day I came across a small group of men gathered around an object on the sidewalk in front of Farman's drugstore. Pushing my way in among this bunch of grown men, I found that several had something in their ears much like a doctor's stethoscope with tubes leading to a strange-looking contraption. My eyes caught the movement of machinery inside this object, and my ears soon told me that sounds were emanating therefrom.

As you may have guessed, the "contraption" turned out to be an Edison Phonograph—the first that had ever been on display in Rushville. You had to put a nickel in the slot to listen in on one of the five earphones, but there were leaks in the transmission, and by getting real close I could hear the record being played almost as well as those who had paid for the privilege. The record was announced as "The Burning of a Negro in Paris, Texas," and it was a horrible thing which I doubt if the authorities today would permit to be made or sold. The record was not a flat disc, but a cylinder—just like those still used on some types of dictating machines. It began with the announcement of the title of the selection, and then you heard the words "An Edison Record."

I don't recall exactly how long it was after this that I saw my first telephone. It wasn't much to look at, but the use that could be made of it was what interested me. In those days, a man with a big ranch had quite a problem and some job riding the fences to see if the cattle had broken through during the night. There were spreads so large that it took many days of riding to complete the circuit; and because of the ever-present threat of cattle break-throughs or some-body cutting the wire, the trip had to be repeated con-stantly. But the native ingenuity of one of the ranchers solved the problem for all. He got his hands on a telephone with a few batteries and hooked the instrument to the mid-dle wire of his fence—the strand that was bound to be broken if harm was done to the fence at any point. By talking into the transmitter and holding the other part to his ear, he could hear his own voice if the fence was still okay.

I had heard of sheep herders getting so lonesome that they would talk to themselves; but never before had I known of a man in his right mind talking to himself just to be assured that nothing had happened to his fences. The only fly in the ointment was that when it rained for a few days the fence posts got soaked through, thus shorting the circuit, with the result that the rancher's voice went into the ground somewhere along the way.

Though I may not live to see the day when mechanization becomes total, at least I was on hand to witness the humble beginnings of "push-button ranching."

V

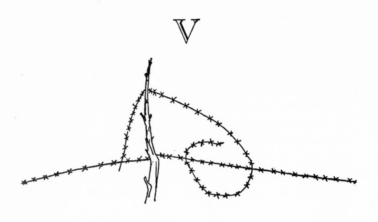

PINE RIDGE AND THE SANDHILLS

Education without opportunity

Aᶠᵗᵉʳ ᵐʸ ᵍʳᵃᵈᵘᵃᵗᶦᵒⁿ I just had to find a job somewhere, so I invested my last two dollars in a stage
ticket to Pine Ridge. I had been told that the Government
brickyard there would be taking on men because they were
about to start making four million bricks to be used in the
construction of the new Indian School buildings.

On the stage with me that morning were four members
of the Sioux tribe—a fine-looking young man and three
young women far too well dressed and refined in appearance to be called squaws by any decent white man. We five
were the only passengers, and exchanged quite a lot of talk
throughout the journey. It developed that they had just finished seven years of study at Carlisle, the Indian school back
in Pennsylvania, and they told me more about chemistry,
physiology, and higher mathematics than I had any idea

there was left for me to learn. They were now well-educated young people, and impressed me as amply equipped to take their place in any community as useful and responsible citizens. But against them was the fact that they were only Indians, members of a minority race.

The young man and I decided to see more of each other, so when I had secured work at the brickyard I managed to get him taken on also. He turned out to be a fine worker, and the boss missed him very much when he was transferred to the staff of the Government hospital. Someone had learned he knew chemistry, and he was put in charge of the dispensary.

We met frequently, and on Sunday afternoons and evenings took long walks during which we discussed things in general and the outlook for his people in particular. While he never complained about any treatment he had received from white men, he did feel very bitter about the way the soldiers had handled the burial of his slain friends after the massacre at Wounded Knee. Probably he was away at school when this took place, but he had been told enough of the details to be very sensitive about the whole subject.

This is the account he gave me of what had taken place after the Battle of Wounded Knee:

"I know my people were wrong to take part in the uprising but their very existence was threatened, and they felt they had to do something. Yet I cannot help but be shocked and saddened by the manner in which they buried our dead after the battle was over. First, they scraped out a long trench, wide enough to receive a body laid crosswise and deep enough so that several layers of bodies could be laid in, one on top of the other. Then privates of the United States Army placed a row of Indian bodies across the bottom of the trench, covered them with old army blankets, and then put down another layer of bodies, lengthwise of the trench. And so they continued until the dead were nearly level with the ground. Then the dirt was shoveled on."

You will have to make your own decision as to the truth of this description; my friend, at least, was convinced that his facts were the correct ones.* My brother Ab, who went all through this battle and saw much of the fighting, later told me that soldiers had been given fifty cents for each Indian they buried in this fashion.

Now what became of the three little Indian maidens? The brickyard where I worked was only a short distance from the fenced-in compound where all the business of Pine Ridge Agency was administered, so I went up to "town," as you might call it, quite often, and on several occasions saw one of the three wheeling a baby carriage which contained the offspring of Bob Pugh, the issue clerk at Pine Ridge. She had quickly secured a place with the Pughs, and so far as I know stayed there very happily. I also caught an occasional glimpse of another of the girls who also had found employment with a white family in the Agency colony. She seemed quite well adjusted and no doubt was making a valiant effort both to retain what she had learned at Carlisle and to try to climb a bit higher on the social and economic ladder. I sincerely hope she did.

For several weeks I lost track of the third girl, and then to my surprise and horror she was brought to the brickyard by her father, who offered her to the rougher type of worker for twenty-five cents a "lay-in." She was no longer clean and lovely and had totally lost her spirit: life meant nothing to her now. It appeared that she had been unable to get any work or find a home at Pine Ridge, so had to go on up north somewhere—I believe to a place called Stinking Water Creek. Her folks made fun of her appearance and attire and refined manners, and the work of disintegra-

---

* See pages 215-216, last paragraph of note on Wounded Knee.—
Editor's note

tion began as soon as she arrived at what they called home. Then her degenerate father got his terrible idea of making money out of her, and—in the words of a then-popular song—

> He made her what she is today.
> I hope he's satisfied.
> He dragged her down and down
> Until the soul within her died.

In justice to the Indians, especially the Oglala Sioux, I must state most emphatically that this is the one and only case of parental abuse I ever knew of, either from personal experience or hearsay during all my time out in that part of the country. Also, I found the Oglala Sioux to be far more modest in exposing their bodies and far more chaste in their sexual behavior than could be said about a comparable group of white people of that day.

A tragic story like this girl's was a natural consequence of our failure to follow up our once rather elaborate educational program by providing suitable opportunities for the nation's wards. Instead, the knowledge and culture derived from their schooling was wasted for lack of nourishing tasks and a respectable social status.

As an additional example, I might cite an incident which occurred some thirty-five years later, in the early 1930's, when I was again back in this section. I wanted very much to obtain an Indian headdress, or war bonnet, as a trophy to be awarded each month to the salesman in my organization who had made the best record. My plan was to put the bonnet in a nice case and send it to the winner who would then be "Big Chief" for thirty days—and no doubt would get quite a kick out of showing it around, have his picture taken in it, and so on. But I soon learned that it was far easier to find a good salesman than to get my hands on a headdress or any other authentic item of Indian regalia.

My search took me to the general store of old Noah Moss in Clinton, Nebraska, not more than six miles from the sod house we had built back in 1885. Noah Moss was the patriarch of that district—he'd been running his store long before I left Sheridan County. I thought if any man would know where I might obtain Indian trappings, it would be old Noah. His advice was to give up the search, for the latest raid of "head-hunters" from Hollywood had stripped the entire community of everything remotely resembling an Indian curio. In Hollywood these tribal and family treasures were used to portray the Indian as a savage killer or, occasionally, as a sort of Tarzan-type Olympic champ or circus performer doing fantastic things that were rarely, if ever, done in real life.

Noah introduced me to a young Indian, a Carlisle graduate, who had served in the armed forces during World War I. "My friend," he said after I had explained what I was looking for, "I am quite sure you will not find a single example of an authentic Indian headdress in this country. I know of but one really first-class outfit, and that one is mine. It consists of a chief's headdress, war bonnet, tail piece, scalp belt, and anklets." This sounded mighty good to me, so I asked him what he wanted for it. "It is not for sale," he said crisply. "This was handed down to me by my father." So that was that.

We talked of other things and finally I asked him what he was doing for a living. "Pickin' spuds," he said. Here he was, an educated man, and the only work he could find was digging potatoes! The current rate for this work was $3.00 a day, with camping privileges, firewood, and all the potatoes the family could eat. But you can't pick spuds when there are none to pick, and after a few weeks at most the job would be over for another year. Then there would be nothing to do but return to his humble home on the reservation and try to survive until some other odd job turned up.

Thus the red man has always been treated—living on a miserable handout basis when no work was available, and when he was given work it was mostly the kind that the white man did not like to do. Maybe this clipping from the Gordon, Nebraska, *Journal* of April 22, 1959, will give you a little idea of what our past and present treatment of the Indian has resulted in.

Police Court

Randolph Sun Bear, intoxication; $40 and costs.

Oliver Sun Bear, intoxication; $10 and costs.

David Good Weasel, intoxication; $10 and costs.

William Eagle Bull, theft; $10 and costs.

Freda Spotted Bear, (1) intoxication, (2) disturbing the peace; (1) $10 and costs, (2) $10.

John Bird Head, intoxication; $15 and costs.

Verine Bear Robe, intoxication; $10 and costs.

Byrdie Spotted War Bonnet, intoxication; $10 and costs.

Madeline Eagle Bear, intoxication; $15 and costs.

Curtis Bear Robe, intoxication; $10 and costs.

Romeo Pretty Hips, intoxication; $15 and costs.

Julia Pretty Hips, intoxication; $15 and costs.

Steven Kills Enemy, no driver's license; $10 and costs.

Indian characteristics and customs, based on my first-hand observation of the Oglala Sioux in the '90's

Ever since the Creator made Eve out of one of Adam's ribs, the male of the species has claimed superiority over the female on the grounds that he furnished the material for her manufacture. So far as I know, this overlord status has prevailed pretty generally until fairly recent times. Now, of course, the average man hardly knows where he stands in a lot of things.

But among Indians that I have seen and known there was never any question about the buck being boss over his squaw and all the rest of his often large family. It was he who did the hunting and she who cooked and did what housekeeping was needed around the tipi, and who literally bore the burdens of everyday life. Many times have I seen a buck go strutting down Rushville's main street headed toward the Indian camping ground just across the F.E. & M.V. tracks, perhaps leading a pony that he brought into water at the town pump, and after him at a respectable distance his squaw trudging along with bent back and straining muscles, toting a bale of hay.

When a party of Indians hit town, it was the squaws who made camp. They would jerk the tipi poles out from under the wagon and quickly put them in place, with the poles crossed for strength; then in one swift movement run the canvas around. This operation would be reversed when they departed. In a shorter time than you would think possible the outfit would be loaded and ready to leave; and when the Indians were gone, so were all evidences of their presence. Never were there any objectionable odors or litter in and around the Indian camping grounds. Whatever tiny scraps of meat, bone, or bread were not consumed by the human members of the party would be devoured by the many hungry dogs that were always with every Indian group.

The squaws were accorded very little opportunity to participate in amusements and sports. Although the men's activities were mostly carried on out of sight of the whites, I have on a few occasions seen young Indian braves swimming, but I never did see one without a breechclout on. Racing, wrestling, and contests with the bow and arrow were main diversions of the Indian boys. In one of their games, a lad would shoot an arrow as far as he could, aiming it so that when it lit it would stand upright in the ground. This would furnish a target for the others, who would shoot in turn, and the one whose arrow came closest would get all the other arrows as a prize. This seemed to me fair, as a different boy made the lead-off shot each time. They also played a game on the order of our horseshoe pitching, except that they use the polished shin bones of animals instead of horseshoes. This game followed along the same lines as the arrow-shooting contests.

In virtually all of the various Indian dances the men did most of the performing. In preparation, they would undress and daub their bodies and faces with colors of every hue—green, yellow, red, black, white—the ghastlier the better. After the cosmetics had been smeared on, they would don breechclouts, headdresses, tail feathers, anklets, and whatever oddments they had in their wardrobes which they felt would add to the occasion. The men's dances were very active and hilarious, with lots of leg work and circular movements, all done to the accompaniment of the tom-tom; and the faster the drums beat, the faster the dancers moved up and down and around in a circle. The dancing of the squaws was as quiet and ladylike as that of the bucks was violent and dramatic. You saw no gaudy colors, no fancy regalia, just a group of drab, impassive womenfolk dressed in plain skirts cut from old blankets, sometimes with a few simple ornaments on them.

Generally speaking, the squaw dances reflected the position they occupied in the family and the tribe. I have heard it said that in the early days, when the Indians were still lords of the plains, there was a dance which the squaws were supposed to keep up until the braves returned from a buffalo hunt with lots of meat or perhaps as victors in a battle with another tribe. This could very well be true because some sort of discipline must have been necessary to keep the squaws in the humble, uncomplaining frame of mind which they outwardly displayed. There might have been family spats inside the tipi, but I never knew of any.

I couldn't say from personal knowledge whether or not the Oglala Sioux practiced polygamy. I have many times seen a half-dozen squaws of various ages in the company of one buck, but whether these were extra wives or just daughters and sisters I didn't know. My information on Indian marriage ceremonies is so limited that I'm not even sure if they had any; but I do know they had very definite and distinctive ideas about the burial of the dead. However, in spite of the many reports of the custom, I doubt if there were many Indians who would kill a precious pony and tie it to the grave so that it would be handy for the deceased to mount and ride away on when the Great Spirit gave him the come-on signal. On the other hand, tree-burial—placing a wrapped body in the crotch of a tree—was quite common until the white man's rules and regulations put a stop to it.

Torn Belly: Sioux Screwball

Many writers and public speakers have been telling us for years that the Indian is stoical, taciturn, and utterly devoid of the emotion of pity. Some even have held that the Indian cannot shed tears because long exposure to wind and hot sun has dried up his tear glands. This I doubt very much—although come to think of it I have never seen a teardrop on the cheek of either a squaw or papoose, even under the most distressing circumstances. I know that they do at least weep inwardly, as I can testify to hearing their loud lamentations in camp at Rushville when Buffalo Bill's contingent of braves was awaiting the train to take them east. In connection with their emotions, I learned one single word that seemed to fit all occasions which called for the expression of sorrow, disappointment, or anger. This word was *O-tay-heh*, and it might be used in case of death, of failure to obtain permission to leave the reservation to hunt and fish, or of anger—much as we civilized folk would cuss somebody out. Sometimes to make their anger more emphatic they would add a tailpiece, making the word *O-tay-alo*.

Whatever the real truth about the Indian's temperament, I found my friend Torn Belly a most invigorating contrast. How or where he got his name I can't tell you—like the Negro singer of a later period "I didn't ask, he didn't say, so I don't know." Anyway, we met while I was working up at Pine Ridge.

During my first couple of weeks at the brickyard, while work was in its preliminary stages, I drew the job of gang cook—and incidentally my dozen or so "customers" told me I did right well at it. My kitchen was just outside the fence enclosing the Pine Ridge headquarters, near which was an abandoned dugout that I found handy as a food storage place. I had dug a fire-pit over which I placed a slab of steel about a quarter-inch thick and three feet square. On this I fried steaks and made coffee and flapjacks. My only mistake was when I tried to cook beans. From boyhood observations at home I knew that to loosen the hulls you boiled the beans in soda, but I failed to wash the soda out before I put them in a big pan to bake on the hot steel slab. The result was a dish that was a thing of beauty but no joy whatsoever. On top was the most gorgeous crust done to a golden brown, but when the boys broke through it and sampled the soda-filled interior there was a great weeping and wailing and gnashing of teeth.

After we had scalped off the drying field, making it nice and level, and were ready to set up the brick-making machinery, the working force had to be greatly enlarged. A big cook shanty was set up and two Negro cooks installed to do the culinary chores, so I no longer served as combination chef-and-laborer. Among the many new workers there was a goodly sprinkling of Indians, hired to do the heavy work. Torn Belly and several of his brethren had the assignment of wheeling the clay from its hillside pits and dumping it into the pug mill to be thoroughly ground up and made ready for molding into bricks.

My job was to stand beneath the pug mill—with its cold, slimy water drip-drip-dripping down my neck—and lift each mold as it came rolling up toward me from the sanding machine, turn the mold over, tap it just enough to remove most of the sand from each of the six brick openings, and then insert it in the opening beneath the rapidly descending plunger to be filled with six bricks. All this at the rate of nine molds per minute. If I missed by a split second or got the mold in a bit cockeyed, there was hell to pay and no pitch hot.

The first evidence of Torn Belly's original kind of humor came one day when he felt like taking a rest—he trundled his load up to the pug mill and dumped the whole wheelbarrow in. Naturally, this stopped all operations until the wrecked barrow could be cleaned out of there, and old Torn Belly got his nice rest.

About every two hours the whistle would blow and the

order shouted out to wash molds. This was necessary because in spite of the sanding that I had been able to do,
some clay would still adhere. If it were allowed to accu-
mulate, the wet bricks would not dump out of the molds
when the men carried them out to the drying field to lay
out in rows for sun-drying before going to the kilns. During the necessary time-out for mold washing we were all
more or less at liberty, and old Torn Belly used to carry on
talk with me as we passed each other on the field. One
often-repeated question I remember well, because it was on
most of our minds all day long. This was *"Muzis-kahska-
tonah?"*—What time is it? (*Muzis-kahska* = time; *tonah* =
how much?) Then I would look up at the sun, study it
with all the wisdom I was supposed to possess, and reply,
"Ahkee-waszhee, sem-okees" if I thought it was half-past
eleven.

When the new cooking arrangement was put into effect,
an order was posted that the table nearest the kitchen was
reserved for the highest-ranking supervisors, timekeeper,
paymaster, etc. From here on it was catch-as-catch-can between the ordinary white workers and any of the Indians
who could pay the meal price of a quarter (or *Showkla*).
On the first day of this new arrangement when the noon
whistle blew we all rushed down to White Clay Creek to
wash up. Washing was a simple matter, and hands could be
dried quite well by stripping leaves off the willows growing
conveniently along the bank—even grass would do to dry
hands on. But neither grass nor leaves were quite the thing
for face-wiping, so for that we reverted to the time-hal-
lowed practice of using our shirttails or sleeves. Then came
the scramble for seats and eats, and when the stampede was
over I found myself at the second table with old Torn Belly
at my side.

The tables were covered with plain oilcloth and seated
about twenty; there were tin cups, and iron knives, forks,

and spoons. The meal of meat, boiled potatoes, and maybe another vegetable if any were available, was served help-yourself-style, excepting the coffee which one of the colored cooks poured.

Torn Belly said not a word and seemed to be getting all the food he could handle until his coffee was poured, and he wanted sugar for it. He looked longingly at the sugar bowl, which was out of his reach, and then spoke in his own language first, just as a tryout. "*Sha-hum-pah*," he said in an ordinary tone of voice. Nothing happened, so he said it again quite a bit louder, and still the men kept right on feeding their faces. When a third effort was equally fruitless, he experimented with "Pass the sugar"; and that time got it pronto.*

I came to know my fun-loving friend quite well and gave him a royal welcome when he showed up in Rushville some months later. It was from Torn Belly that I got most of my knowledge of the Sioux language—the meanings of its various expressions and combinations of words.

The Sandhills

From the date I graduated until I left Northwestern Nebraska for good in 1898, I seldom stayed put more than a few months at a time. Possibly I may have had in mind hunting for the pot of gold said to be at the end of the rainbow, but my real basic motive for moving around was to insure daily contact with the contents of the kitchen kind

---

* Although the author gives no more examples of Torn Belly's humor, it is apparent that he remembers him vividly as the perpetrator of many comic acts. Mari Sandoz has suggested that Torn Belly may have been a Contrary, a member of the *heyoka* or thunder cult. The actions and words of the *heyokas* were always contrary to what normally would be expected. See the note on page 221.—*Editor's note*

of pot. In other words, I was interested in eating regularly and so I went where jobs were. From Pine Ridge I went down to Mosler and Tully's ranch in the Sandhills, then to Smith's sheep ranch near Clinton, and then to clerk at Ecoffey and Steel's store in Rushville, which is where I was at the end of 1896. It was during this year and the next that I became better acquainted with a goodly portion of the strange region known as the Sandhills.

To my knowledge no one as yet has by pen, brush, or camera produced anything like a realistic picture of this at times almost spooky yet fantastically fascinating section of Nebraska. Covering about 18,000 square miles, the Sandhills section occupies all of Cherry County, a large part of Grant and Hooker counties, and the northern part of Garden County almost to the Platte. To the east and south of these roughly outlined borders, the Sandhills fade out into a mixture of sand loam or black sand, and then into quite firm black soil. To the west, also, the soil gradually firms up and becomes steadily more rugged as you near the Wyoming line. After a few miles' travel to the north of Gordon and Rushville you come to white clay cliffs fairly well covered with pine trees: west and northwest of here lie the Dakota Bad Lands, and still farther to the west are the Black Hills. These spots—the Bad Lands and the Black Hills —are well known to tourists but the Sandhills have been pretty much overlooked.

As you travel over these hills, you are apt to get the impression that some titanic contractor with labor problems decided to give up the thankless task of building the world and ordered his men to dump everything and pull out. But what appears to be a vast and uncertain wasteland has been organized by nature on a quite workable plan. In addition to the huge piles of sand, the main features of the terrain are the numerous alkali lakes scattered through the hills, and the system of alternating wet and dry valleys that prevails throughout the central part of the area. This alternating arrangement provides a wet valley with a permanent and usually quite good-sized lake in one spot and, not too far away, a dry valley which will produce a good crop of hay every season. Usually a dry valley will fill up with water in the late fall and winter, but hardly ever does enough water seep in, or enough rain fall, to make a permanent lake. Every now and then, though, the boys have to hurry to get the hay crop cut down, cured, and stacked around the rim of the valley before rising water stops their work or makes it much more difficult.

In a wet valley the lake is surrounded by a plentiful growth of rushes, maybe some good-sized willows too. Wild ducks and geese find such spots ideal tourist camps in their seasonal flights from north to south and back. In valleys like this the owner can build as elaborate a home as he might desire with the assurance that he will always have a good water supply for his livestock and plenty of soft, cool water for his household. He can grow the finest fruits and vegetables found anywhere in the semisand soil that rises up as you move away from the lake. In the heavy soil still farther back from the lake, alfalfa in enormous quantities is grown for hay.

Out where the real sand begins you will find little growing except a peculiar grass, the like of which I have not seen elsewhere.* It is not buffalo grass, neither is it bluestem or any standard-named brand. It is just grass, but the steers love it and thrive on it. During a mild winter, cattle on the sandhills range prefer to feed off this nature-cured grass. Hay can be saved for emergencies like a blizzard or exceptionally heavy snowfall, which make closer-in feedings necessary.

Either by accident or design—who knows?—the north

---

* Probably *Boutelova gracilis* (HBK) lag.—*Editor's note*

side of many of the hills slopes gently upward, and can be scaled with comparative ease by cattle, horses, or men; but the south side generally is very steep. Thanks to the fact that the range of hills runs northwest to southeast and the valleys tend to follow this line of direction, the rancher providing feed for his herd can haul hay from stacks nearby and pile it along the bottom of the south side of this protecting hill. Most of the bad winter storms come from the northwest or at the extreme air current shift from the northeast, so the cold wind and blowing snow pass well over the heads of the feeding cattle in the valleys some hundred feet below.

During the summer this outdoor feed yard with its winterlong fertilizing is likely to produce a field of sunflowers ten feet high, with flowers on them that make the pride of Kansas, which calls itself the Sunflower State, look like a boutonniere. After the first heavy frost, when their seeds fall, comes the Thanksgiving feast for the grouse. Just about dusk they come walking along talking to each other, headed for protection as well as a banquet under the tall and densely grown sunflower stalks. Everyone knows that sunflower seeds are good for fowl, and the grouse is no exception—in fact, the grouse of these parts is as near like a farmyard fowl as any other bird I know.

While there may be some monotony in the size, shape, and general layout of the main body of the Sandhills, there is an almost infinite variety of things to be seen, enjoyed, and eaten. In some sections where the soil has firmed up a bit and there is little chance of shifting by wind, you will see whole hillsides covered with gorgeous, fragrant-smelling sweet peas, usually pink or lavender. Here and there you come across patches of different flowers of many colors, sizes, and shapes, each appearing in its own season. The most majestic of these is the yucca—which we unlettered natives pronounced "yooka," not "yuhka"—and which is also called soapweed. (Just why, no one has ever explained to my satisfaction, as it in no way suggests soap.) * It resembles the scrub palmetto of the South in that it is made up of spines projecting out like rays of light, only the yucca's rays are much more distinctly separated. These branches grow at least two feet in length and are so fibrous that the plant might well have been named the ropeweed. After many wagon wheels had passed over them, I have seen them ground into a stringy fabric several feet long as tough and strong as most any commercial cordage material.

The yucca's crowning glory, however, is the bloom rising up out of its heart, like the plumed helmet of a knight of old. Standing above the spines at least two feet and bearing on its crest a cluster of brilliant milk-white flowers, this plant can be seen at a considerable distance, especially since there is often no other colorful flora in the areas where it grows. In the late summer its flowers give way to seed pods, also very curious and interesting. When fully developed but still green, each pod is a little larger than a hand grenade of the type used in World War I. (It was great sport for us youngsters to gather a supply of these and see how far we could throw them. They were quite heavy, and sure did make good tossing material.) When fully ripe and very dry, the pods crack open and the seeds drop to the ground either to be eaten by some hungry bird or—while still clinging to a part of the old dried-up pod— to be blown about until they settle down in a new location and the next spring begin raising a new family of soapweeds. The life span of the yucca plant seems to be many years: I don't recall ever having come across a dead plant except where it happened to be growing in a spot that had

---

* The roots contain a saponaceous matter which may be used in place of soap. The method of preparation is to strip off the bark and then pound up the pulp. An excellent lather is produced when warm water is added.—*Editor's note*

been chosen as a path for a ranch wagon. After repeated crushings by many loaded wagons, there you would find a dead soapweed.

The most fearful and peculiar thing about the Sandhills is the blowout in which the whole top of a hill is speedily transformed into something very like the crater of a volcano. There are several ways in which a blowout may start —for example, pulling up a sand-cherry plant could easily start one if the wind is just right; or a pawing steer may have unloosed enough turf to make an opening for the wind to whip up another. I personally have seen such a birth: First a whirl of sand, then a larger, funneling movement; and then, as the rapidly enlarging crater helps to create a bigger draft, the real fast work begins. In the space of a few hours a blowout can develop which would spell death to any steer who might happen to slide down it. Also, a cowpuncher riding along attending to his job can easily get too close to the brink of this unseen hazard. Of course, most likely a man would be missed and a search would locate him before he perished, but the fact that I have seen a goodly pile of bones of many different sizes at the bottom of many older blowouts does prove that they are a very real danger to both man and beast.

When it comes to saying what the Sandhills look like, it would require quite a stretch of the imagination to speak of them as beautiful. But they are fascinating to study from different angles—showing variegated colors when viewed from one direction, and appearing drab and stolid from another. They can seem weird and menacing, steady and prosperous looking, dull and dispirited. While never so terrifying or inscrutable as the great American desert lying farther to the west and south, there is some family resemblance. But the Sandhills country is more inviting to man and more dependable, as if it had a sincere desire to settle down, become civilized, and take its place in the world of progress.

One thing I can say for sure: Travel where you may, you will never find another region like the fantastic Sandhills of Northwestern Nebraska.

The last of the Longhorns

In the middle of the haying season, 1896, Eddie Wasmund and I went down to the Sandhills to get work. I drove my pony and cart and Eddie rode his horse, but every now and then he would tie his mount to the cart and ride with me for company. We were about twenty-five miles south of the Niobrara, approaching a cut between the hills, when out of nowhere not two hundred feet away there appeared the biggest drove of Longhorns I have ever seen.

The Longhorn is not an easy critter to describe. You may get a little idea of his general appearance if you can imagine a body somewhat like a sunfish, a head like the one a four-year-old child would produce if told to draw a cow, and a very flabby, stringy neck hooking this head onto the body. It was his horns that gave this animal his distinctive appearance: many a steer had a set that measured five feet from tip to tip. Since this tended to make him look over-balanced, you would wonder how he could handle such equipment, but when you saw him in action—especially when he was mad about something or at somebody—you would stop wondering. He knew what they were for, and he knew how to use them.

The cut in the hills was only about fifty feet wide, so Eddie and I saw only the front ranks of the herd, but even so it was an awe-inspiring sight. With their long shiny horns gleaming in the midsummer sun and their bodies so close together, they gave somewhat the effect of a Greek phalanx excepting that their spears were held horizontally.

I don't know how Eddie and I looked to the rest of the Longhorns, but the lead steer was not impressed favorably. He began to indicate displeasure by pawing up the loose sand and tossing it over his shoulders, scaring Eddie's horse, who broke loose from the cart and ran off. Fortunately for us, some fifty yards away he stopped to look around a bit. Obviously one of us had to go and get him and after some discussion we decided that Eddie would stay with the cart while I went out to catch his mount. Eddie had brought along a shotgun and could use it better than I.

When he had his gun loaded and cocked and ready to fire at the first steer who charged, I got out of the cart. By the time I was about halfway between the cart and the loose pony, the steers apparently had made up their minds that I was the guy they wanted. Lowering their heads and pawing the sand, the leaders started to move toward me. But I was not fooling around any in catching and getting aboard Eddie's horse, and we both were back at the cart before the herd had time really to get worked up to anything.

When we were all set again and started driving through the bunch, they very obligingly parted to each side and let us pass between them. It was then we got our first idea as to the herd's size: there must have been several hundred of them.*

It was the last herd of Longhorns we ever saw. They were being driven to Merriman to be dehorned before being shipped to Iowa, where the gents would be converted into the makings of beef stew or dried beef while the ladies would be bred to Shorthorn bulls. And so it is that today

---

* "A herd of 'several hundred' Longhorns wasn't worth mentioning. Several thousand, yes. Several hundred are only a *bunch* of cattle."
—*Mari Sandoz*

the Texas Longhorn is nothing but a memory in the hearts and minds of a few old-timers who knew them when they roamed the plains of the Panhandle.

Ranch-hand recreation and rascality

Unless you have lived long enough to remember a world without radio and television, you may find it hard to realize how few things there were for a ranch hand to do in his spare time on a ranch back in the '90's. Most of the men couldn't read very well, and even if that had been what they cared to do there was little or nothing for them to read. And supposing a man had some cash—which was seldom the case—where could he go? He was at least forty miles from a town of any size; there were no shows, not even moving pictures; and only now and then a dance—to which few, if any, of the men would be considered welcome. Of course there was always card-playing, but about half of the gang didn't enjoy it. So what did this leave?

Well, there was stick-pulling, a game for two, a sort of variant of so-called Indian wrestling. You sat down on the ground with your feet braced against the feet of your opponent and both of you grasping a heavy stick, usually the remains of a broken pitchfork handle. The object was to keep pulling until one of you pulled the other enough off balance to be completely upset. Once in a while there would be some friendly rasslin', but that so often led to a fight that on most ranches it was taboo. By and large, for entertainment there was really nothing much but broncho riding and playing practical jokes on the tenderfeet who showed up to join the work force, which happened most often during the haying season—July, August, and part of September.

On the Mosler and Tully ranch, I found some twenty fellows of as many different sizes, shapes, and attitudes. The modern expression about "men from all walks of life" didn't apply in that place and time. There was but one walk of life, that of the common laborer who worked with his hands, with tools and simple machinery. Most of this labor force, like myself, also could do a fair job of riding even though we couldn't be classed as broncho-busters—nor did we want to be so set apart. However, in most every other category we did stack up pretty well with the wranglers.

The chief hoss-wrangler was in a class by himself when it came to taming wild horses, and the Mosler and Tully ranch had some thousand head of these animals. After they had been broken to ride and to harness, they would be teamed off and issued to the Indians as part of the Government plan to make farmers out of the nomadic Sioux. Among this bunch of horses there were always some likely prospects for a worthwhile tussle with their would-be rider. So it became a custom, of a Sunday afternoon, for the men to chip in twenty-five cents apiece, and then take turns choosing a horse for our wrangler to ride. The purse usually amounted to around $2.00, which was not bad for a minute or so of time.

The sporting element for us depended on our ability to pick a nag that would give the wrangler a run for his money. One day my choice fell on a large, rather bony, flea-bitten roan that would weigh around a thousand pounds and had what looked to me like fire in his eye. He was quickly roped and then blindfolded to be saddled and made ready for his rider. I think the gunny sack must have slipped a mite so that the roan had peeking-room: at any rate, when the saddle had been gently lowered on his back and the cinch tightened just enough to hit his belly hairs, he didn't wait to think matters over. Breaking away from his handlers, he began bucking his way around the ten-

[165]

foot plank corral. The saddle swung down under his body and became a kicking target for his hind feet, and the drumming of his hooves on the saddle convinced everyone, including the saddle's owner, that it was being ruined. The as-yet-unmounted broncho-buster sang out, "You can have my silver-trimmed saddle for fifty dollars!"

Before he had a chance to "Dutch auction" it down to twenty-five, the horse had been roped again and this time the men double-checked the blindfold and everything went according to Hoyle. The rider got safely in the saddle, the blindfold was jerked off, and hell really broke loose. This big animal, supposedly destined to become a plow horse for domesticated Indians, had all the makings of a present-day rodeo star. Three times he bucked his way around the stockade; then, seeing strips of daylight between the two-by-fours that formed the corral gate, he leaped high in the air and came down right in the middle of the gate, smashing it to the ground. The rider was able to leap clear, so when the horse was on his feet again our man was all set to resume the contest. But now the beast was out in the open spaces, no longer hampered by the confinement of the small corral. Bucking, jackknifing, sunfishing, he soon reached the barbed-wire fence and there—because of the danger of death or serious injury for both horse and rider—the boys roped him down, and the show was over. Neither man nor animal had won; but neither wanted any more testing.

The very next Sunday another tough-looking horse was selected to be ridden for a purse of about the same amount. But this one trotted off dutifully like an old milk cow, and we got no thrills for our money.

The arrival of a tenderfoot was looked forward to, especially if he seemed a bit more sissified than the mill run of such visitors, because of the opportunity to play practical jokes. It so happened that not very far from our ranch house was an alkali lake. If you have never seen such a lake, you have missed an unusual sight, and if you have never been swimming in one, you have missed quite an experience. You get the sensation of swimming in very light oil, but without any greasy effect, and it is most enjoyable until and unless you get your hair wet. What happens then is what makes the alkali-lake swim so popular as the basis of a good practical joke.

In the instance I'm thinking of, the victim was a friendly sort who had been with us only a few days and seemed to be holding up his end of the haying work quite well. But the boys wanted fun and that was his day to be "it." We all went swimming together and after a little urging the greenhorn decided to give himself a shampoo. The shampooing part was easy; but the rinsing was another matter entirely. The more he tried to wash out the rich lather, the more of a suds he worked up, until finally his head resembled nothing so much as a five-tier wedding cake all frosted and ready for the reception. By the time we had gotten back to where there was some fresh water, the alkali froth had begun to harden and only with great patience and help from the jokers did the victim manage to get rid of that handsome accumulation of suds which outdid any you can see on a modern washday detergent commercial.

Come to think of it, even though we had neither radio nor TV then, between our broncho-busting and our alkali-lake hijinks, we did have our own form of both horse- and soap-opera.

More Torn Belly

As I started to think over the following incident before typing the actual words, there began running through my head a song that someone sang at one of the Literary and Debate Society gatherings way back in 1886 or so. Though the melody is clear in my own ears, I can only give you the words. This is how they went—you can make up your own tune to fit—

> One bitter night in winter
> As the wind blew fierce and wild,
> A girl looked in our window,
> A weary, hapless child.
> Then Grandpa whispered "Baby,"
> And tottered to the gate.
> To save her from sin, he brought her in
> To the fire in the grate.
> Then keep the fires burning,
> 'Tis charity's brightest flame,
> Reminding of the evening
> When the orphan Mary came
> So weary, cold, and helpless,
> With Grandpa from the gate.
> For him she kneels, her prayer she yields
> By the fire in the grate.

'Twas just such a night as this in the winter of 1897, and the wind was blowing fierce and wild as one of those vicious Nebraska blizzards raged. My job was to keep the fires burning—not in the grate, but in the large wood stove in the rear of the store of Frank Ecoffey and Yellow Bird, in Rushville. This was necessary to prevent liquid supplies from freezing; also we had bottled bluing and some canned goods that could swell up and burst if they got good and frozen. So I was staying late that night to keep the stove well stoked and build up a surplus of heat that would carry over until morning.

The store where I was now employed had for many years belonged to William Alexander, but when that fine family moved away from Rushville others took over, and eventually it became the property of Ecoffey and Steel—Steel being the white-man's name adopted for business reasons by the Indian named Yellow Bird. Since he had a marked fondness for alcohol in any form, whenever we got advance word of one of his periodical visits we would hide as best we could all the vanilla, lemon extract, and other preparations with a high alcohol content. Invariably, Yellow Bird would crack off the bottle necks and gulp down the contents of as many as he could locate. Frank Ecoffey, on the other hand, was from a high-class French background and had no annoying or destructive habits, with the possible exception of his hospitality. He had placed the sole responsibility for running the store on Frank Jennings, yet he was constantly urging him to close up the place for a week or so and drive up to the Ecoffey ranch home some miles north and east of Gordon. He had plenty of room and lots of food, and a very good time could be had by all. You can gather from this that the Rushville store was merely a sideline with him.

All alone in the store on this stormy night, I had nothing to do but keep the stove well filled. Time was hanging heavy when, as in the song just quoted, "the girl" looked in the window—only it was not a girl and I wasn't to know who he, she, or it was for several minutes. Ecoffey and Steel's was a typical small-town store: entrance in the center front, with a display window on each side of it. My chilly night caller did what many Indians always did—shaded his eyes against the north window and tried to see through the heavily frosted windowpane. Then he tried the same thing at the south window. Finally he tried the door, much to his surprise found that it could be opened, and in he came.

Seldom have I seen such a sample of poverty and misery. He was ill clad, ill fed, and just plain all around badly in need. As he came toward me from the front of the store,

I could tell that he was an Indian buck, but he was so covered with snow, frost, and ice that this was all I could be sure of. His only protection against the bitter cold and the snow was a threadbare blanket which he had wrapped about his body. His feet were encased in some canvas salvaged from a discarded tipi, and his hair was done in two braids with a piece of red flannel tied at the end of each. Snow and ice were lodged in the folds of his scanty garb to make life just that much more miserable for him.

After my friendly greeting of *"How kolah,"* he drew up to the red-hot stove and started to thaw out. It was then that I recognized him as Torn Belly, my old brickyard friend of the year before at Pine Ridge Agency. Clearly this reunion had to be celebrated, and the only way I could do it was to give him something to eat.

In those days we sold lots of cheese which we bought in wheels and from which we cut large hunks whenever a customer said, "Gimme a nickel's worth of cheese and crackers." My storekeeping experience came just after the era of the cracker barrel; we bought our crackers in a big wooden box about the size of the thirty-dozen egg cases still used in many towns. Our liberal serving of cheese meant that there were always a lot of good-sized hunks lying on the cutting board, and there were also a lot of scraps of ham and bacon or salt pork handy. So when Torn Belly had gotten pretty well warmed through, I spread a sheet of wrapping paper on the counter nearest the stove and loaded it with cheese and meat scraps and plenty of soda crackers. Then Torn Belly piled in. Never in my life have I seen any human being wolf down so much vittles in so short a time.

When the inner man had been satisfied—probably for the first time in many moons—the old fellow gathered up all the leavings, wrapped them in a none-too-clean red bandanna, tied the four corners together, and said by way of

explanation, "Squaw." These leavings were to be her reward for keeping an eye on things at the tipi while he was
out on the town looking for food.

Now it was my turn to take over, and with Torn Belly
at my side walked all over the store while he named in
Oglala Sioux the various objects I pointed at. I don't recall
his giving me Sioux words for any fabrics: in buying these,
the average customer merely pointed at the one in question
and asked the price—"*Muzis-kah-tonah?*" However, I did
gain quite a few additions to my Indian vocabulary and
learned the Oglala Sioux method of counting, which follows:

One	Wah zee
Two	Noh pah
Three	Yominy
Four	Toh pah
Five	Zop ta
Six	Shock-o-pay
Seven	Shock-o-ee
Eight	Shock-o-loza
Nine	Num chee ga
Ten	Wicks chiminy

When you reached ten, you said ten and one; and when
you got to twenty, it became two times ten or "*Gosh-pop
nohpah.*"

Torn Belly also told me that the only word for grease
was "*Wee-glah,*" so when the settlers began to move in,
bringing with them butter, lard, and axle grease, the Indian
had to make up words to fit. Thus butter became *Wee-glah
Tibliska* or cow grease; lard was *Wee-glah Koo-koshya* or
pig grease; and because of its color, axle grease was *Wee-
glah Soppa*, black grease. His word for crackers was *Wee-
up-sock*, which he said meant flour and water mixed and
cooked on both sides.

When I ushered him out about midnight we both felt the hours had been well spent. He got his belly full and I got my mind full of Indian words (which have never done me any good, but they have done me no harm either). And that was the last I ever saw of old Torn Belly.

The Indians always paid more for what they bought, and received less for what they did. Typical of the former were my instructions for figuring up the total cost of goods bought by an Indian. For instance, if the purchase was six yards of calico at fifteen cents a yard, I was told simply to say *"Wah-zee"* or one dollar. The alternative would have been to say *"Showkla-Yominy-goshpop-sem-okeese"*—literally "Three quarters, ten, and a half of ten." How much easier and simpler to say *"Wah-zee"* and let it go at that. This was not done for the deliberate purpose of cheating, so they told me, but to avoid giving the Indian a small piece of money, such as a dime, in change. Many would have punched it and sewed it on a blanket or a shirt as an ornament.

I am sure there is no business man in the Indian country today who would admit to anything like this practice, much less try it under present-day economic conditions. Also, I expect there isn't one Indian in a hundred who would recognize the words I have written. All I can say is they are put down the way I "heered" them then and remember them now.

VI

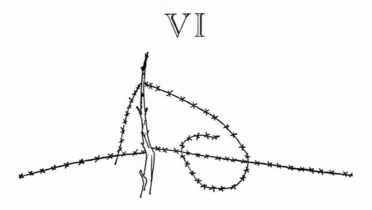

RUSHVILLE, WATERTOWN,
WHITE CLAY, AND POINTS EAST

*Our second and final journey in a covered wagon,
this time a round trip*

AT THE START OF 1897, the O'Kieffe clan in Rushville
had dwindled down to Mother, Minnie, and myself.
Brother Grant and his family, as I have told, had moved to
Butte, Montana; and Ira, when last heard from, was in
Sheridan, Wyoming. Ab and George had pulled up stakes
and gone to Upper Wisconsin where they were felling trees
for a big logging company.

Ab had married a Catholic girl and both she and her
mother went along with them. The mother-in-law had all
the characteristics that inspire mother-in-law jokes and was,
in addition, very strict in the practice of her religion. She
told Ab he could not eat meat on Friday, but logging is
hard work and builds up an appetite, and Ab made up his

[173]

mind to eat meat whenever and wherever he could find a chunk of steak to sink his teeth in. This started a ruckus and after some weeks of continuous harsh criticism Ab and George decided the only way to get some peace was to leave all the argument behind. So when they had a reasonable amount of money coming to them, they both signed over their pay to the womenfolk and that very night headed out of there.

George worked wherever he found anything to do until the next summer. Then he "throwed in" with a friendly hobo, and they beat their way to the North Dakota harvest and threshing fields. There they accumulated quite a lot of ready cash, as such things went in those days, and when the cold winter winds started sweeping across North Dakota's treeless plains, the two pals rode the rods south, looking for a warmer climate and more favorable working conditions.

They got to Omaha but found no employment there, so they hit the rods again, making for the western country where George at least knew somebody and where they would have a place to hole up for the rest of the winter. But a few miles out of Omaha George's pal slipped and fell between the cars, and George saw his body cut in two pieces. This was the end of the hobo trail for him. At the nearest depot he spent most of the cash he had on him for a ticket to Rushville, and from there went to our farm.

There he stayed until, in the spring of 1897, we decided to drive across the country to Watertown, South Dakota, where Mother had some halfbrothers. Being now the senior member of the family as far as the male element went, George had to go along and handle the logistics of the trip. This he did in a most proficient and appreciated manner, for the tragedy of a few months back had taught him quite a lesson about life and our dependence on one another.

Because this was to be a sort of exploratory trip and we

expected to return in a few months, there was not a great deal of work to be done in getting ready. Our tree claim, now proved up on and properly deeded to Mother, was sold along with some odd lots of livestock for enough money to finance us. The old harness-maker and dealer in Rushville, George Figge, fitted us out with a new wagon cover, with bows to hold it in place, and a new set of harness for the team (no longer good old Charley and Jim, who had long since gone the way of all horseflesh). We also took along a very fleet and neat little Indian pony just to have some form of transportation in case of emergency.

None of us were excited as we drove up to and on past Gordon and then headed east, almost backtracking the route that brought us to Sheridan County in 1884. Excepting for Ira, our personnel was the same as before, but now we had ample clothing and bedding, and we would be passing through some quite well-timbered country so there was no fuel problem. I think we also had some cash money.

With fresh horses and happy hearts we made very good time each day; our speed was at least twice as fast as on the way out from Johnson County. There were good places to camp each night, and our sleeping arrangement was about as before—Mother and Minnie inside the wagon, George and myself under the tarpaulin slung over the wagon tongue. The second night out we camped pretty close to the railroad tracks, forgetting that our horses had never seen a train. They had been staked out for the night and George and I were sound asleep when the express came along. The lights streaming through the coach windows, the whistling, and the thundering roar as the iron monster bore down on our camp was too much for our country-bred team. They yanked up their lariat stakes as if they were toothpicks, and away they flew. Fortunately one of them passed close to where George was just crawling out of bed in his long underwear. As the lariat rope whipped by, George grabbed on and held tight, though he was dragged for a good hundred feet through a number of cactus beds.

That was the only bit of excitement as we moved on eastward through Nenzel and Valentine. Soon we hit the gumbo-soil section, and after a heavy rain the sticky mixture of clay and sand clotted on the horses' hooves until they became great round balls. Because of the threat of broken ankles we had to stop frequently to knock the gumbo off.

We reached the Missouri River at Wheeler and when we pulled up on the west bluff I must say that I had never in my whole life seen so much water.* The river had backed up from some place below Sioux City and at the spot where we were supposed to cross it now stood at over a half mile wide. The water was a rich coffee-with-cream color and there was very little current, not over a mile an hour. It looked more like a lake than a captive river.

An enterprising old codger had rigged up a raft for a ferry and fitted it with one of the early-model gas engines —the first I had ever seen. It was a one-lunger, and it sure did cough and spit when finally started. The ferry boat itself was just a floor of planks laid on a few logs, with a ring of ropes to keep things and people on board. The noses of the team stuck out over the bow of the old ark and our wagon box was even with the stern, while our little pony had to be tucked in alongside the wagon.

When we were well out on the broad bosom of the wider-than-usual Missouri, Mother asked the old pilot how long it would take to get across. "All depends, lady," he said. "If the engine breaks down, no tellin'. If it don't, only a few minutes."

---

* That was the year 1897 and, as some of you may recall, it was a year when the old Missouri backed up to an unheard of depth and width.—*Author's note*

Naturally Mother's next question was what happened if the engine *did* break down. "Why, lady, we just float down the river till we get it fixed."

After landing at the improvised port cut out of the hillside, we were off to Mitchell where we crossed the James River—the Jim, as they called it then. The James had not taken on as much backwater as we had found at Wheeler, and although some fifty feet of the approach was a foot deep in muddy water, the steel bridge across was still intact and usable. From Mitchell we rolled on to Watertown, in the extreme northeastern part of the state, arriving in early June.

We found lodging in the home of Grandma Waite, who was in some way related to our Mother. George soon got a job working on the bridge that was being built across the Red River, some six miles out of Watertown; and I went to work in the general store owned by our uncles, Charley and Andy Gayman.

Among the new things I came across in Watertown were buildings of what they called grout construction. The work is started with a cribbing of small wood members, probably not over 2″ x 2″, which are set much in the way a small boy might build a house of corncobs, excepting that there were two sets of these wooden members, placed about nine inches apart. A very light mixture of lime or cement, sand, and lots of mud is poured into the crib thus formed. The mixture oozes out between the side members and soon hardens; then the mess is trowled off and the wall is complete. It is a cheap and easy method of construction, and they thought so much of the idea locally that a five-story hotel had been built this way. When I was in Watertown it was not operating, due to lack of trade.

Another building of grout construction was the saloon run by Ed Lamb, which stood just across the street from the Gayman Brothers store. It was the finest saloon in Watertown, and it surely was a busy place. At least every other day I had to carry over a large box of those little oval-shaped oyster crackers that were so popular with beer before the era of pretzels and popcorn. The cracker boxes were just the size of a thirty-dozen egg case, and many farmers bought or begged for them to use as egg carriers from farm to town.

The street between Lamb's saloon and our store came to a dead end about a half block to the north, and the entire cut-off space was occupied by a huge yard where an implement company displayed its stock. One fateful day the management received the first steam engine for farm use that had been delivered to those parts, and an expert from the factory came along to show how the thing worked and put it through its noisy paces. Having delivered a box of oyster crackers to Ed Lamb's saloon, I was back in the store watching from the window as the ponderous steam pachyderm lumbered around the implement yard. I was called to the rear of the store just about the time the engineer brought the beast to a snarling stop and let off a mass of hissing steam. A few seconds later when I came back to the window there was nothing but a cloud of white dust where once had stood Ed Lamb's saloon.

The material in these grout walls was so light that when the sudden stopping of the engine, with its tremor, was added to the shaking already received, the total was just too much—the building did not topple over, it merely wilted and fell into the basement. Soon a crowd of men was frantically digging out the customers, none of whom were badly hurt, though almost smothered in lime dust. Only the bartender was killed: his neck had been broken when the huge back bar fell on him, forcing him down on the bar counter.

"Grout is fine for a building," an old-timer said when it was all over, "but only if you have another house built around your building to keep it from getting wet and then collapsing when it's dried out."

Everything went well in the store until one day Uncle Andy took my hide off for an error in the order of Mrs. Baysinger, a pet customer. It was not my mistake, but Andy had been drinking pretty hard of late so he had to be right and I had to be wrong. I resented the injustice and since I had money in my pocket, I up and quit right then and there.

In a day or so I had a job with the B.C.R. & N. Railroad [Burlington, Cedar Rapids, and Northern], later a branch of the Rock Island system. Our crew was building concrete culverts which had just begun to replace the old wooden ones, and my particular assignment was down in the caisson used to create deep foundation spots for each supporting pillar. Being down there among snails, pollywogs, and slime, cold and wet all the time, brought me a case of what was diagnosed as typhoid fever and I was sent home and put to bed. Although I had been ordered to stay there and recuperate for several weeks, it wasn't long before George—in his usual masterful older-brother role—told me to quit being a sissy and get up and go back with him and work on the bridge gang. My very first day on the job I had to take a twelve-foot back-dive into the Red River in order to escape being struck by a heavy beam which would have sent my brains splashing in all directions.

After working a few weeks more we packed up and made the return trip to Sheridan County. The James River had receded at Mitchell, and there was a fine corn crop in the bottom land where a few months before there had been deep water. At Wheeler the change was even more spectacular: way up on the hillside we could see the roads we had used in the spring to reach the ferry. I believe those roads were as much as fifty feet above the normal river bed.

By a rather strange coincidence, our second and last covered wagon journey ended at Gordon in the cold November dusk at almost the same day and hour we had driven in some fourteen years before.

White Clay School

I brought back from Watertown a few fresh items of knowledge, such as that it is hard to work for relatives and get along with them, and that the water of the Red River is quite cold in mid-October. Also, I knew the words of two new songs which were rapidly sweeping the country over—"Ta-ra-ra-ra-boom-de-ay" and "There'll be a hot time in the old town." No doubt this is not the kind of educational matter that is taught in Teachers College, but nonetheless my next job was that of teaching school.

In our section of the country with its motley population from almost every nation in the world, only a small percentage of the settlers were greatly interested in any form of education beyond thinking that every male, at least, should learn to read and write and cipher a little bit. Hence the requirements for qualifying as a teacher were not too strict. A First-Grade Certificate was a rarity and a Second-Grade Certificate none too common; in fact, much of the country-school teaching was done by holders of the Third-Grade Certificate, the test for which almost anyone could pass who had even the slightest education. It was this latter that I sought and secured, and in a few weeks found myself on the stage headed for my new school on White Clay Creek about halfway between Rushville and Pine Ridge Agency.

On my arrival I was greeted with the word that the schoolhouse had only recently burned to the ground, so we all had to pitch in and put up a new one. We did this rather quickly since logs were not hard to get from the nearby pine woods. Soon the roof was on, the floor down, the door and a few windows in place, and all was ready for school to take up.

For my work I was to receive $20.00 per month and was to "board around"—that is, one week at one school director's home, the next week to another's, until all three homes had been given the task or pleasure of entertaining the teacher, who was quite some punkins in those days. But sometimes personality overcomes custom, and I never left my first boarding place, the home of Nicholas Lehman, located just across White Clay Creek about a half mile from the school. Here I lived with "Nichlous," as he was called by Mrs. Lehman, a fine, busy, and very happy hausfrau, and their brood of some eight or nine children.

The Lehmans ran a truck farm and did quite well at it, raising vegetables and poultry which they sold at Pine Ridge headquarters. Some weeks before I had arrived they had butchered nine big fat hogs, so the place was teeming with liverwurst, blood sausage, and pigs' feet. Moreover, Mrs. Lehman was a most versatile cook and the best soup-maker I had ever met, not excepting my own wife of later years. When the mercury was somewhere around thirty degrees below the red zero mark on the thermometer and we came running across the creek bottom from the schoolhouse at noon, we would head straight for the kitchen, the heart of all family activity. There in the center of the oilcloth-covered table would be a huge yellow bowl, as big as a baby's bathtub, filled with steaming hot soup—cream of tomato, maybe, or vegetable with onions, or beef *mit* noodles. At each of our places would be a smaller yellow bathtub which we would fill with soup ladled out of the tureen by means of a wooden spoon almost as big as a toy shovel. Lots of soup and plenty of homemade bread made a noon meal that was hard to beat.

An event on my very first day in the Lehman home set the stage for my permanent residence there. Their home was a big log affair, divided in two parts with a runway between. (I believe today the more refined folks call this kind of passage a breezeway.) Here was stored harness after it had been oiled up for the next season's use, corn ears that were being dried for seed, and other miscellaneous items. I had arrived an hour or so before the noonday meal, and was seated in the front room or, as these fine old German folks called it, "*Die andere Stube.*" This room was used only for funerals and the occasional entertainment of outsiders; the family used the kitchen for food, rest, and local visitors. The furnishings of "the other room" consisted of some old-style but comfortable chairs, a horsehair sofa, and a marble-topped center table on which rested a stereopticon with a pile of pictures of Niagara Falls and other scenic wonders. There were no books, papers, or magazines—not even a Sears catalog. So I took a trip around the world via stereopticon and thus passed a very happy half hour. Then little Tillie Lehman, with her pigtails and pudgy little figure, entered the room. Coming as near as she felt she dare, she said, "*Herr Schulmeister, essen ist fertig.*"

I immediately arose and went to the kitchen where the kindly Mrs. Lehman met me by saying, "*Ja*, ve now got to be careful vat ve say in the face of *der Schulmeister*, he knows German." My denial did not settle the argument because she came right back, "For vy den did you know to come by de kitchen?" I replied that I knew Tillie wasn't saying Merry Christmas as it was not the time of year for it, and as I was hungry I got up and followed her in. Either my logic or my ignorance of German must have appealed to Mrs. Lehman, for she sent word to the other school directors that "Ve haf decided to keep *der Schulmeister* all der time." And there I stayed most comfortably and happily during my term at White Clay.

My bedroom was a small cubicle just off the kitchen, with no window and no other door than that to the kitchen. I slept on a huge featherbed with another one on top of me as covers, and despite rumors about the unhealthiness of this kind of bedding my slumbers were peaceful and I never caught anything like tuberculosis.

Among my pupils was a big awkward fellow brought to school by his Grannie from somewhere up in the white clay hills. His first name was Frank, he said, and his last name sounded like Lenna. He didn't know how old he was, nor did his Grannie, but I guessed he must have been in his mid-twenties. Neither had any idea how his surname ought to be spelled, so in order to give him a name to be proud of as well as to provide him with a challenge in learning to spell it, I entered him on the books as Frank Leanagh. I do believe he was the proudest young fellow in the west when he was able to write it out.

The rest of the pupils were the typical assortment you would find in a country school of that time and region, some brighter than the average, many too dull to classify. But the Babby children, two girls and one boy, were the prizes. Grace, the oldest of the trio, was at least two years older than I and had spent several months attending the Holy Rosary Mission School just out of Pine Ridge Agency. She was quite a good musician, and had a grand piano in her log house up the gulch from our school. It was by far the largest musical instrument I had ever seen—in fact, it was the first piano I had laid eyes on. Up at the top of another canyon lived Old Man Robinson, who owned a fiddle on which he performed right well. Quite often on Sunday evening we went to the Babby home and Grace and the old fiddler would perform for us. The old man could not read a note, even if there had been any music to read, but they played real well together.

Grace's father was a highbred Frenchman and her

mother was an Indian of unusual attractiveness. Some people said she was of the Wyandotte tribe, but no one could explain how she got way out in the Sioux country and Mr. Babby never enlightened them. Grace's brother and sister were good students and well-behaved, both in school and out.

It might interest you to know that I became quite fond of Grace. She had every virtue I thought desirable or necessary; and after I went to Omaha we corresponded for a year or so. Then she wrote me a pathetic little note saying that she had decided to marry an Indian because "if I marry a white man and we don't get along, he will say, 'Get out, you're only an Indian anyway.' So I feel much more sure of my future by marrying one of my own race."

"Mr. O'Kieffe, meet Mr. O'Kieffe!"

During the final months of my life in Rushville I supplemented my store-clerking income by managing the local opera house. Today I cannot recall who employed me or what they paid me for this none too busy or important position. As I have mentioned, the rather high-sounding name of Opera House had been given to a long hall on the second floor of Rushville's largest brick building. The first floor and part of the second were occupied by county and town offices.

The place that was mine to manage and fill as best I could with acceptable entertainment had at one end a quite adequate stage, a drop curtain with advertising on it, a couple of scenic rear curtains, and a few flats. The stage was illuminated by a half-dozen kerosene lamps fitted with curved tin reflectors to throw the light back on the stage. For seats, we had about 150 ordinary kitchen chairs which could be lined up around the walls when there was a dance on tap. When there was a show and we wanted to sell reserved seats, we would chalk numbers on the floor and lay out the chairs by rows and sections.

One day I was approached by a very fine-looking, well-dressed man who said he was Dr. B. H. Westphal, and that he wanted to rent the opera house for two weeks to demonstrate the efficacy of his Herbs of Health and Wonder Oil. After he had signed the permit application with our town clerk and paid the modest fee, he asked me to come along with him to the hotel to meet his singer.

When we walked into the lobby of the Commercial Hotel, he took me across to a man seated on the other side of the room. "Mr. O'Kieffe," he said, "meet Mr. O'Kieffe."

This coincidence of names meant little to me: I had heard of O'Keefes as policemen, bartenders, and prize fighters. But the other man became interested as soon as he knew how I spelled my name. "Charley O'Kieffe," he said thoughtfully. "Father's name John?"

"Yes."

"Mother's name Mary?"

"Yes."

"Married in Portage, Wisconsin?"

"Yes."

"Hell, you're my brother."

That's how simple it was to meet a brother I had never seen before and in fact didn't even know existed.

I took him out to the house where we were then living, and Mother recognized Jack at once. It seems that in his boyhood he had been stricken with a disease like our present-day polio which shriveled up his lower limbs. He could only get around with a pair of crutches, but from his waist up he was the most man I have ever met: shoulders that would have been the envy of any fighter or wrestler and a size-nineteen collar. I was told that if he could get back against a wall so he could brace himself upright, he could lick most any two men. However, it was his voice that got him in the entertainment field. It was of good enough quality for the legitimate musical stage, but of course in his crippled condition that was out of the question. The only work of this kind he could get was with the medicine show, where he did quite well even considering the small pay doled out by most of the road companies.

When the curtain went up on the Rushville first night, Dr. Westphal opened the show with a few impressive remarks about what his Herbs of Health could do and had been doing over the years, also how his Wonder Oil had cured many folks of deafness. Then the curtain went down and in a few minutes it rose again and there was Jack seated in a big chair down-front stage center, with his long Prince Albert coat draped around his withered legs. His violin and his banjo were placed on two chairs flanking him. He started to sing, and I must say that he had the finest and most vibrant tenor voice that I had ever heard. With a few exceptions, none more pleasing in tone or volume has come to my attention during the long years since.

After Jack sang several numbers came the *pièce de résistance*. Mrs. Westphal appeared in the center of the stage, dressed in a wonderful and daring black formal gown. It was cut dangerously low in front for the good folk of my day, but she covered some of her nakedness by wrapping several ropes of pearls around her pretty white neck, and on various fingers where good form said she might wear them she was sporting some fairly hefty diamond rings. But her job was not to show off herself, or her gowns, or her jewelry. The featured exhibits were two benches, one on each side of the stage, on which were about sixty two-quart mason jars containing tapeworms that had been removed from sufferers who took just one package of Herbs of Health. Each jar was labeled with the name and address of the former owner of this particular worm, and the date of its delivery from his interior.

If you have never seen a tapeworm in person, you have not missed a great deal because they look something like the discarded skin of some long snake. Or they might be compared to a long slice of tripe peeled rather thin. Each specimen had two black dots supposed to be eyes and giving authenticity to the claim that these were real tapeworms removed from real people. As additional proof, before the Westphal Medicine Show closed in Rushville, Charley Hagel, our town blacksmith, had been relieved of a hundred-and-six-foot worm that he did not realize he possessed. Naturally this fine fellow was added to the collection. For several weeks Charley went about looking like a corpse, thin, pale, and very weak; then he began to pick up and when I saw him last was the picture of health. Of course we all know that "there ain't no sich animal" as the tapeworm; but Charley Hagel could give you quite an argument.

When Jack left Rushville with the show, I asked him to write now and then. "Never wrote a letter in my life," he said, "but I'll see you some day." And we shook hands and parted.

Four years later I was serving as Car Accountant in the Missouri Pacific local freight depot in Omaha when one evening the phone rang and my boss said it was for me. This came as a shock because I had never been called by telephone in my entire life, and did not even know how to use the darn thing. When I finally got myself under control and properly arranged to listen, I heard, "Hello, Charley, this is Jack. I'm over in Council Bluffs and I want you to come and have dinner with me." You bet that as soon as I finished my day, I mounted my bicycle and headed for the Bluffs, some three miles to the east across the Missouri River.

There I met the same folks I had seen in Rushville. After a very good dinner we chatted for a half hour, and then the show went out on the street to start business. For that night they had a very large rig—either a brougham or victoria, I am not sure which, but it was the biggest carriage I had ever seen except maybe brother Grant's famous rockaway stage coach. It was drawn by a beautiful pair of white horses, and altogether the outfit gave a sort of royal coloring to the show.

The program was about the same as before, but being out-of-doors it drew a type of spectator not usually found in places where the audience was restricted by limited space. On this occasion I had a good opportunity to witness the Wonder Oil treatment for deafness. It began with Dr. Westphal shouting at the top of his voice at an old man from the audience who had climbed up in the carriage. Next, the "patient" was well massaged behind each ear and the ears themselves cupped in the palms of the doctor's oil-covered palms, and the demonstration ended triumphantly with the doctor talking to the smiling old gent in an ordinary tone of voice. Hooray for Wonder Oil!

After the show I cycled back to Omaha, and Jack and his company moved on. Our next meeting was some five years later when I was manager of the local branch of the Republic Oil Company in Sioux City, Iowa. Mother and sister Minnie were living with me in a neat little cottage just a few blocks west of the post office. My tank yard and warehouse and a small office were located on the bank of the Missouri adjacent to both the Illinois Central and North-Western tracks, and my walks to work took me in between the passenger depots of these two lines. One day while hurrying home for lunch, I ran smack-dab into brother Jack. I urged him to come home with me for lunch or at least to say hello to Mother, but he said the show was now traveling in its own private car and in a few minutes they would be leaving en route to Oklahoma for the winter months. So I went along to their car, and found the whole bunch all well and more prosperous than before. We talked a few minutes, then parted once more.

Ten years later I was spending some weeks in Marion, Iowa, when at General Delivery one day I was handed a bunch of mail addressed to brother Jack. I told the Postmaster that it was not for me, but that the man to whom it was addressed was my long-lost brother, and I would appreciate it if he could stretch the rules a bit and tell me where it was to be forwarded. A couple of days later he told me the mail had been ordered sent to Strawberry Point, Iowa. I immediately called the only hotel there and was told that Jack had checked out the day before, giving no destination.

That was as close as I ever came to seeing him again. It is hardly possible that he is still living as he would now be around one hundred, quite an age even for such a man as Jack.

A couple of points still bother me: Are there such things as tapeworms any more? And did the people who bought Herbs of Health so freely do so because they wanted to be healed or because they liked the Holland gin with which the herb brew had to be mixed? It took a good pint of Holland gin to preserve properly and make palatable those Herbs of Health. (Wonder Oil had to stand on its own powerful limbs: it was for external use only, you rubbed it on; and I am sure that not even a Sioux Indian with his mighty appetite for anything alcoholic would ever wish—or dare—to take a second nip of Wonder Oil.)

There is one other thing I speculate about: Do you suppose there is a chance that some time I might hear St. Peter say, "Mr. O'Kieffe, meet Mr. O'Kieffe"?

Last words in Rushville

When a poor young man from the West starts East to make his fortune, his feelings are usually supposed to be in one of two categories: either he is full of doubts and sadness or else he is cocky and sure that from now on the world is to be his oyster. Well, I guess the first category is the one which better describes how I felt when I left Rushville, since the only kind of oysters I had ever had any contact with were those obtained when I helped the ranch hands at what we crudely called nutting time. This refers to the operation by means of which rambunctious little bulls are changed into docile, easier-to-fatten steers, the beginnings of those luscious steaks for which Western Nebraska is famous. The residue from this unsexing operation when carefully washed in cold water, dipped in corn meal, and fried in deep fat becomes Mountain Oysters—a tasty and most satisfactory substitute for Cotuits or Lynnhavens to cowmen half a continent away from saltwater oyster beds.

On my last day in Rushville I wandered about like a lost soul. Mother and Minnie had moved to Wayne, Nebraska, to live on a farm with sister Belle and her family, and a few friends were all I had left in the town and community where I had lived from the age of five to nineteen. As night came on and one by one the stores closed, I dropped in at George Evans's jewelry store and there he sold me a lottery ticket on a $100.00 Columbia bicycle. (It would have cheered me up considerably if I could have foreseen that I was going to win it, but I was not notified of this until some time later.) Then I went down to the depot and took a seat in the dimly lighted waiting room, though it was still early and the eastbound train was not due in till after midnight.

No one else was in the waiting room, and the only other person in the whole building was the night operator, George Newman. To while away the slow-moving hours I took my recently purchased $3.98 Sears Roebuck mandolin from its canvas case and began to pick out the strains of "Swanee River." But I had barely reached its beautiful banks when George bellowed, "For Gawd's sake, cut out that infernal plinking!" This was hint enough for me, and I repacked the mandolin.

George's words were the last spoken to me in Rushville, unless you count the conductor's "All aboard." I was the lone soul to take advantage of this invitation, in fact there was no one else on the platform. Then the highball whistle sounded and away we went into the dark night.

From buffalo chips to banking,
with business college and a beer garden in between

A stray catalog that I happened to pick up led me to the unguided program of getting a business education. On the second day of my life in Omaha I gave all my money to one of the biggest business colleges in the state for a Life Scholarship. This provided that I could attend classes as long as I desired, then go out and work awhile and, any time I felt the need, come back for a refresher course. I also got a job washing silverware in the restaurant of Jimmie Huston, featuring "All You Can Eat For 10 Cents." For my lodging, I had a room in the home of Charley White, who owned and operated the New England Bakery. In return for the accommodation I took care of their driving horse, milked their little Jersey cow, and put ice in their refrigerator twice a week. The ice I had to dig out of the sawdust in the ice house on the back of their lot.

When necessary, I mowed the lawn and did other yard work.

I had been going to business college just ten days when I came down with typhoid fever again, and have never been back to college since. Fortunately my case was mild, and still more fortunately Mrs. White and her two fine children had taken quite a fancy to me. I was urged to stay right there until I got well and had secured some sort of job.

It turned out that my scholarship was not transferable and of course the men who sold it to me were "very sorry, no refund, but you are always welcome to re-enter classes" —and similar soft soap. Later on when I became better known in town and securely anchored in the Methodist Church where these two business-college brothers also were active, I told them they would either have to let me sell my unused scholarship, or else! They consented, and I sold it to a young fellow who became proficient enough on the typewriter to be the champion speed-writer of the entire West. Thus it all worked out very well: the college was proud and glad, and so was I in addition to having my money back.

Meanwhile, how about a job? A pretty tough question because 1898 was the year of the great Trans-Mississippi Exposition in Omaha and everybody was looking for day-time jobs so they could see the Exposition at night. By sheer luck, I met Nade Howell, a friend from Sheridan County who also had come to Omaha to carve out a career. Together we walked the streets vainly seeking any sort of employment.

Over the years I have never known it to fail: it is always decided to repair the principal streets of a city just when the largest crowds are expected. Well, Omaha was no exception: the repair gangs had started on Sixteenth Street where there was the heaviest traffic. It was summer—the asphalt was hot, the pushing crowds were hot, and so was the temper of those doing the work. Therefore, you can imagine what sort of a reception Nade and I received when we approached the foreman and asked for a job. I had just spent several years in a rough-and-tumble area, and from childhood up had heard many expressions that a growing boy should never hear, but this old sea-pirate boss of the asphalt-patching gang spilled out to us words that I did not even know existed and have never heard since. The sum total of his outburst was that he had the choice of ten red-blooded he-men for every job open, so why bother with snotty-nosed kids?

Later that day Nade and I went down to Mickey Mullen's Beer Garden on Capitol Avenue just off Sixteenth Street, said to be the toughest place of questionable entertainment west of Chicago. We had heard Mickey was looking for spry young men to sling beer every night, and in fact he gave us quite a sales talk on the possibilities of profitable employment in his establishment. The pay was ten per cent of the bottled beer we sold to the yokels who crowded in to watch the cavorting of the half-naked girls, who would then sit down at the tables and permit the customers to buy them beer at $1.00 a bottle. The price was so high because the place might be raided at any time and profits had to be garnered while the garnering was good.

We arranged to return at six P.M. to get our aprons and big nickel-plated badges. Then I walked up to the Merchants Hotel where I could usually find someone from the West to talk to—and I surely needed to talk now. Passing through the bar just to see what was on the Free Lunch menu, I ran into Johnnie Jones, the Rushville lumberyard dealer who also was Joe Thomas's partner in the bank. Two people who have only a nodding acquaintance back home often will greet each other like long-lost brothers when they meet in a strange town, and so it happened now. Johnnie forgot that I was merely "Mrs. O'Kieffe's little boy

Charley"—he saw me as a real personality with whom conversation would be most welcome.

He told me that Joe Thomas had been made cashier of the Union National Bank in Omaha, and knowing that I needed a job real bad he took me over to Joe's bank where I was made most welcome, as Joe had not forgotten the friendly ways of the West. He had been looking for a young man to learn the banking business his way, and had become disgusted with city smart alecks who had been sent to him. Result: I went to work the next Monday morning at $20.00 a month.

So began a new chapter of my life—from now on I would be Mr. O'Kieffe and never again Charley O'Kieffe of Rushville. But if I am ever reincarnated, I sure would like to be sent back to Sheridan County among the buffalo chips and tumblin' weeds just to learn how such things would appeal to me after having had a taste of life under more favorable conditions and in many different surroundings.

HOW WE CAME OUT

Mary Elizabeth Gayman O'Kieffe (1841-1925)

In her eighty-fourth year, Mother passed away peacefully in the Old Soldiers Home at Burkett, Nebraska, near Grand Island. She had broken both her hips some years before, and the good folks in the hospital had fixed up a neat little reading table on which she kept her Bible from which she read almost continuously. Her arms and hands were in good condition, so she could turn the pages. I had been to visit her a year or so before her death and she was very happy, comfortable, and well cared for. When I left, she pleaded with me not to come back. "I am in my right mind now, but when you come again I may not recognize you. I'm all right here and have my plot all selected and my headstone ready, so please keep the money the trip would cost and use it to educate your lovely children."

Belle O'Kieffe Auker (1863-1917)

I have already told how Steve started on the road to success in Sheridan County. When the question of educating their children came up, Steve and Belle decided to trade their entire holdings for a big farm in the Nebraska corn belt, a few miles east of Wayne. There the Aukers prospered, becoming important factors in the farming, church, and ethical life of their community. After raising nine wonderful children, each of whom got at least a Normal School education, and having seen her youngest son grow to manhood, sister Belle went to sleep one night not to waken again on earth.

GRANT O'KIEFFE (1866-1940)

Brother Grant was quite an ordinary hard-working man with no great promise and no bad habits to hold him back if there was any place for him to go. But the coming of the soldiers at the time of the Indian uprising, and the favors they granted him, led him into the trap of strong drink which nearly ended his career. After he gave up his mail contract following the Indian trouble, he became field expert for the Deering & McCormick binders, which for the first few years had many bugs in their operation. This kept Grant on the go almost constantly, and at one time he got fed up and went away for several months. It looked as if he had left his family for good, but just when they had almost given up hope he sent for them and they moved to Butte, Montana, where he had a job as tool dresser in the Anaconda Mine. But the sulphur fumes from the smelter made Lu, his wife, ill, so they moved to Creston, Washington, where Grant opened a blacksmith shop. Many years of shoeing with its strain on the back brought on kidney trouble, and we next heard from Grant at Spokane, Washington, where he had charge of shoeing the fire horses. Later he moved to Seattle and got in with the street commissioners, and there he ended his days a fine old gentleman, refined and sober, with countless friends to mourn his loss.

ABNER O'KIEFFE (1868-1944)

Brother Ab must have ended his earthly career along in the fall or winter of 1944, as the beautiful story I quote here was printed on June 12, 1945. Many years before, he had gone to Canada and had written me once or twice from Peace River, Alberta, where he once had taken up a homestead. After his long and rather turbulent career, it made us happy to read the following in the local paper published at Berwin, Canada:

> One of the most pleasant affairs of the summer occurred at Berwin's sports grounds today, when over 100 children enjoyed a free picnic with ice cream, pop, peanuts, and suckers. Between bouts of eating and drinking, races were run, with cash prizes for the winners.
>
> The sponsor of this gala day was the late Ab O'Kieffe, wealthy old-age pensioner. Yes, wealthy—for although his estate could not be counted in thousands of dollars, or even in hundreds, he did possess in over-flowing abundance the greatest wealth of all, the love of little children.
>
> How Ab would have enjoyed it! And we feel he did enjoy it, for although nobody actually saw the tall, straight old cowpuncher stalking about with a crowd of little shavers around him, we all felt the presence of the everlasting spirit which he personified.
>
> The children all thank you, Ab, and they will never forget you.

IRA O'KIEFFE (1870-19??)

Brother Ira was sort of a lost sheep during most of my life at home. We lost track of him for some years, but—as I have told—finally heard from him at Sheridan, Wyoming. The next we heard he had moved to Seattle and had married the daughter of a local butcher. Having acquired the drinking habit during his wanderings, he was taken to the hospital for an appendectomy, but demon rum had done its worst and brother Ira had peritonitis in an advanced stage. He never came out of the anesthetic, dying on the operating table. He left his widow and a sweet little daughter.

MINNIE BLANCHE O'KIEFFE (1875-19??)

Sister Minnie ended her days in a Catholic institution at West Point, Nebraska, where brother George's wife Lillie, who was a Catholic, had found a home for her. My records do not show the date of her death; but when Lillie went there to the funeral the Reverend Father told her that there had not been a person in that home for many years with the sweet and loveable personality Minnie displayed. So, while she did not own much of a mind for usefulness, she did make up for that lack with a kindly, patient, and sweet disposition.

GEORGE O'KIEFFE (1877-1943)

After a long and fierce struggle, aided greatly by his wonderful wife Lillie, George managed to carve out of the south Sandhills a ranch that would have been the envy of any man.

Strange are the doings of fate. Way back in the waning years of the nineteenth century, Lillie Taylor was born in Sheridan County and grew up in the Mirage Flats section (pronounced by the natives "Mir-rage"). In 1902 Lillie started teaching school in that locality, and George meanwhile had settled down at the famous Spade Ranch where he was classed as one of their best hands. At the same time that he was called to Valentine to testify in the Government case against Richards, who was being sued for fencing Government lands, Lillie was there to attend Teachers Institute, and that was when they met. When the Kinkaid Law was passed, allowing a person to file on 640 acres of that questionable sandhills land instead of the usual 160-acre allotment, George became a Kinkaider and a little later Lillie filed on an acreage which adjoined his. While George was not the least bit romantic, he was very practical, and now, by the laws of mutual interest and opportunity these two widely different folks decided to marry—or maybe in this case I should say merge—and they did so on October 6, 1910.

Together they built up a ranch that was a credit to them and to the Sandhills as well. But hard work, no children to grow up and be of help, and the utter impossibility of hiring dependable hands made life on the ranch so unbearable to George that he took to the bottle every time he went into Omaha with a few carloads of cattle. (I can't refrain from pointing out that many of the men around the stockyards are not very helpful in cases like this.) When George and Lillie sold their ranch and moved to Omaha in 1929, the same drinking friends who received him with open arms when he had cattle to sell, now brushed him off; and this heartbreaking experience added to George's thirst. He came mighty close to going over the brink, but one day got mad at himself and threw bottle, pipe, tobacco, and cigarettes out of the window and never took a nip again.

Later George and Lillie bought a big farm on the Missouri River near Tekamah, not so very far from Omaha. Here they lived until George passed away in his sleep February 14, 1943, at the age of sixty-six. He had become the idol of the younger business men of that community, and there never was such a funeral in Tekamah no matter who the deceased might have been. Here was a man with no education, but blessed with lots of gumption and horse sense, whose death brought messages of condolence and tributes from a United States senator, the Governor of Nebraska, congressmen, bankers, and cattlemen from all over the territory in which he was known.

Lillie is still living in Tekamah and occasionally pays us a most welcome visit here in Minneapolis. George's death left her with the farm, and for some years she handled matters most efficiently; but at least every other year the old Missouri took over, and ruin was the result. Discouraged by the Government's failure to make good on its repeated promises to do something, she finally sold the 1,800-acre farm with its great potentialities—and right away the Federal authorities got busy and the flood hazard will soon be a thing of the past.

So once again relief came too late so far as an O'Kieffe was concerned. In the '90's we gave up our hard-won homestead in Sheridan County because we thought we had stood all we could stand—but those who stuck it out developed dry farming, potato culture, and irrigation where feasible —and look where they went!

CHARLES D. O'KIEFFE (1879-19–)

So here am I, the last of the original flock of O'Kieffes. I married my first wife, Serilda Fern Ary, at Forest City, Iowa, in 1904. She bore me two sons and passed away. In 1918 I married Della Cecelia Mueller who bore me a son and a daughter.

My oldest son Charles DeWitt had a daughter Karen and two sons—Charles DeWitt the Third, a graduate of Williams College who has recently finished his Army stint, and Michael, still in high school. My second son Donald, who died of lung cancer September 2, 1955, has left us his two sons, Donald and Douglas, and his daughter Diane. Donald is now in Yale and Douglas has started in Taft School in Connecticut. My youngest son Robert has a little girl, Susan; and my daughter Florence, who married Bill Beeman, has three in her flock—Billy, Jimmie, and Nancy.

In things material I have not been what you might call

prosperous; but I have lived a full and happy life, raising four wonderful children, each of whom has gone much higher on the ladder of success than I have. There is much satisfaction basking in the sunshine of their attainments and sharing at least to some degree the honors they have been accorded. So, summing all things up and weighing the good with the bad, I can say with the Psalmist: "Surely goodness and mercy have followed me all the days of my life. Amen."

SUPPLEMENTARY NOTES

SUPPLEMENTARY NOTES

The principal secondary sources used are *History of Western Nebraska and Its People*, Volume II, edited by Grant L. Shumway (Lincoln: Western Publishing & Engraving Co., 1921); *Who's Who in Nebraska*, published by the Nebraska Press Association (Lincoln: State Journal Printing Co., 1940), which contains a brief history of Sheridan County by B. J. Petersen; *Old Jules* by Mari Sandoz (Boston: Little, Brown & Co., 1935); *History of Nebraska* by James C. Olson (Lincoln: University of Nebraska Press, 1955); and *A Sioux Chronicle* by George E. Hyde (Norman: University of Oklahoma Press, 1956). These sources are hereafter identified by the following initials: HWN = *History of Western Nebraska;* WW = *Who's Who in Nebraska;* OJ = *Old Jules;* OHN = *History of Nebraska;* and SC = *A Sioux Chronicle.*

Information about names of localities is, in every case, derived from *Nebraska Place-Names* by Lilian L. Fitzpatrick

(University of Nebraska Studies in Language, Literature, and Criticism, Number 6; Lincoln, 1925).

Other sources are cited in the text.

Variant spellings of names of individuals have been made consistent in quoted passages, but otherwise the quotations are unchanged.

SHERIDAN COUNTY (page 7)

(Names of persons mentioned by the author appear in small caps.)

Sheridan County, named for the celebrated Civil War general Philip H. Sheridan, was originally a part of Sioux County—a great block of unorganized territory stretching from Holt County to the Wyoming line—which was attached to Cheyenne County for administrative, judicial, and tax purposes.

> . . . Principal Indian tribes in this region before the advent of the white man were the Sioux, the Pawnee, and the Cheyenne. A band of the Sioux known as the Brule Indians lived for some time on Beaver Creek, and here [in 1871] was established the Spotted Tail agency named for their chief. . . .
>
> Spotted Tail agency disappeared after a few years, and in 1874 Fort Sheridan was established on Beaver Creek not far from the agency's previous location. The latter post was discontinued in 1881.
>
> The first white settlement in what is now Sheridan County was made on White Clay Creek, approximately twenty miles northwest of the present site of Rushville. Most of the first settlers took "squatter's right" upon the land, filing later at Valentine after the United States land office was established [in 1881]" (WW, p. 1040).

On 1 July 1885, Governor James W. Dawes proclaimed the new County of Sheridan, "the same being a strip sixty-nine miles long and thirty-six miles wide off the east edge of Sioux County" (HWN, p. 422). These boundaries had been defined by an act of the legislature approved 25 February 1885.

The proclamation named Rushville as temporary county seat; T. B. Irwin, L. E. Post, and J. D. Woods as special county commissioners; and James W. Loofbourow as special county clerk. At a meeting of this board on 25 July 1885, they divided the county into three commissioner districts, Ranges 41 and 42 comprising the first, 43 and 44 the second, and 45 and 46 the third. The county was further divided into ten voting precincts: Wounded Knee, Larrabee Creek, White Clay, Beaver Creek, Hay Springs, Rushville, Gordon, Heywood, Hunter, and Mirage. At the first election called, the following officers were elected: Judge—CORNELIUS PATTERSON; Treasurer—Albert McKinney; Superintendent—S. S. Murphy; Clerk—Abel Hill; Sheriff—John Riggs; Coroner—James F. Tucker; Surveyor—SOLOMON V. PITCHER; Commissioners—T. B. Irwin, G. T. Morey, and J. D. Woods. Subsequently, W. W. WOOD, C. C. Akin, and W. H. WESTOVER made application to act as county attorney, and the commissioners accepted Westover (HWM, p. 422).

A county-seat election was held on 8 September 1885, the four contestants being Gordon, Rushville, Hay Springs, and Clinton. Like many county-seat elections, this one generated great bitterness and much chicanery. Rushville had a plurality but a majority was required, so a second election was held on 27 September. Clinton previously had been eliminated, and on this go-round Gordon fell by the way. At a third election on 3 November, Hay Springs had a majority but

fraud was apparent and the matter was taken into court and the votes recounted. The recount disclosed that Hunter precinct with only forty-two legal votes had brought in 226 votes for Rushville. Even Rushville's own vote exceeded the legal limit by 130. Hay Springs . . . had tallied 243 more votes than voters, and Gordon had cast sixty-five fraudulent votes (WW, p. 1041).

A Supreme Court decision in 1888 finally decided in favor of Rushville.

In addition to Gordon and Rushville (discussed below), two other Sheridan County towns, Clinton and Hay Springs, both organized in 1885, figure in the author's recollections. Clinton, named for Clinton, Iowa, was not a "station" town, which explains why the O'Kieffes traded at Rushville and Gordon, even though Clinton was nearer their homestead. Hay Springs, thirteen miles west of Rushville, is "near the west line of the county . . . and the fartherest west of any railroad town in the county. It has the highest elevation, the same being 3828 feet above sea level" (HWN, p. 421). Its name is an accurate description—Hay Springs lies in the center of a meadow country where the soil is moistened by many springs.

GORDON (page 7)

The town was named for John Gordon of Sioux City, who attempted to take a wagon train to the Black Hills when this part of the country was still Indian territory and closed to white settlers. About five miles from the present location of Gordon, he was overtaken by a U.S. cavalry detachment, his oxen turned loose, and his wagons and freight burned. The lieutenant commanding the detachment was later dismissed from the service for this offense.

Gordon was founded by a Civil War veteran, Reverend John A. Scamahorn. During a visit to Louisville, Kentucky, in 1883 he met Judge J. Wesley Tucker, United States commissioner at Valentine, Nebraska. Reverend Scamahorn was a sufferer from stomach troubles and complications to the extent that the doctors had recommended a "change of climate." Judge Tucker was always an enthusiast for Nebraska, and . . . assured him that northwestern Nebraska was the most salubrious climate in the world. Scamahorn was from a malarial section of Indiana, and a number of his neighbors were with him, and all became interested in the new Mecca of the great northwest.

That autumn, the year of 1883, six or seven of them determined to come out and look it over. While here they ate so hearty and slept so well that they were assured it was indeed a healthful climate, and they returned with glowing reports. During the winter a party of 104 was made up to come west into the wilderness. On March 20, 1884, they left Sullivan, Indiana, chartering cars to Valentine, and bringing along their stock, horses, cows, farm machinery, and household effects.

Necessary funds were a concern to many of them, and not the least of these was the Rev. Scamahorn. He had a cow, a hog, two old horses, and sixty dollars in money. Not enough for carfare for himself and his wife, but he managed to arrange to go as caretaker of one of the cars and that gave him free passage, while the money enabled the wife to travel with the others (HWN, p. 417).

Mrs. Scamahorn added a Holstein cow to the family possessions by trading her "new, upholstered parlor set, which she felt she would not need in her western home" to the cow's owner.

The colony went into camp at Valentine until they could make their land entries, Valentine still being the terminus of the railroad in 1884. From here they made their overland trip to near where Gordon now stands and here most of them made their permanent abiding place (HWN, pp. 417-418).

In 1885 when the Chicago and North-Western railroad was extended west from Valentine, Gordon was made a station.

It was the first settlement encountered after leaving Valentine, the sand hills between not being attractive to early settlers, except those who desired isolation and wide acres . . . . John Crowder brought a second colony from Indiana, and others were arriving in bunches about that time from other states (HWN, p. 420).

On 19 November 1885, a petition was granted by the county board legally creating the village of Gordon. A few days later (28 November) the Rushville *Standard* reported that

Gordon has a population of about 500, two banks, several general stores, hardware, drug, two good hotels, two lumber yards and other necessary industries, with a real live real estate firm to locate pilgrims. It is surrounded by a good country both to the north and south of the Niobrara River. Settlers are coming in rapidly and the business is surprising.

A rousing and accurate description of Gordon at this time may be found in the early chapters of Mari Sandoz' *Old Jules*.

RUSHVILLE (page 7)

The town's name comes from the nearby Rush Creek, a dry stream with a large growth of rushes in the vicinity. The creek was christened by one of the first surveyors in the county.

In October, 1883, about the same time that Judge Tucker [met Rev. Scamahorn], a party of six was made up at Pawnee City, Nebraska, and they, too, came to the high plains region that was destined to become Sheridan County. Twelve miles northeast of the present site of Rushville appealed to them as the land they were looking for. Five of the six took claims in this section, and four of the five became citizens of the county, bringing many others with them . . . . The section held its attractions besides good land—close proximity to the pine ridges for fuel, and abundant good water at from ten to eighty feet below the surface.

North of the present site of Rushville was a community center called "Rush Valley" in 1884. The home-steaders were overflowing the plains west of the sand hills, and as was usual, their first consideration was feed for their stock. Buffalo grass furnished a much better pas-turage than it apeared at casual glance, and it was too short for hay, so the attraction of a natural hay meadows was sufficient to induce first settlers in the matter of lo-cation. "Rush Valley" had some natural meadows. For the convenience of the public, and incidentally the profit in the business, each community early had a store. Two miles north of the present county seat, Henry Crow started a store in 1884, and soon thereafter had a post-office, he being the first postmaster. A mile farther north Cal Weeter started the second store in the "Rush Valley" settlement.

With the coming of the railroad the following year, the new town sprang into existence (HWN, p. 420).

Rushville was legally incorporated as a village on 9 October 1885. Its first school was established that year in the Methodist Episcopal church. Its first newspaper, the *Standard*, already was in existence—"the dean of the press in Sheridan County, it was founded in 1884 by Edward L. Heath, who afterwards served . . . in the state legislature" (HWN, p. 431). At the time of its incorporation, Rushville was still largely a tent town.

On 12 December 1885, the Rushville *Standard* reported that

The editor of the O'Neil[1] *Frontier* visited Rushville last week and through his paper he passes a compliment to our town. Among other good things he says: "We formed numerous acquaintances during the forenoon and were favorably impressed with the town and its future prospects. It is built on a slight elevation, south of the depot, and its business houses are of a substantial charac-ter as is also the business of the town. Its population is about 300. Altogether Rushville and surrounding country is hard to beat and if the town succeeds in getting the county seat (it is the geographical center, almost) they will soon build up a fine town and become a prosperous county."

In view of the fact that the author nowhere makes mention of a doctor—usually a towering figure in early-day communities—it might be well to include here a possible explanation for this omission: "For a long time Rushville told newcomers that the climate was so healthful thereabout that they had to kill a man to start the graveyard" (HWN, p. 421). In fact, the first person to be buried in the Rushville cemetery was William Shafer, who "in some kind of a difficulty" was shot and killed by George Ginger, his partner.

According to *Nebraska: A Guide to the Cornhusker State* (New York: Hastings House, 1939), from its earliest days Rushville has been visited by

> many celebrities, largely because the Pine Ridge Reservation in South Dakota is most easily accessible from this point. Among them were Theodore Roosevelt, Civil Service commissioner at the time of his visit; "Buffalo Bill" Cody; Gen. Nelson A. Miles; John J. Pershing, when a lieutenant in the Sixth Cavalry serving in the Indian War of 1891; Frederic Remington, the artist; and Rex Beach, the author. Calvin Coolidge, while President of the United States, came here to visit Pine Ridge, and was made an honorary chief of the Sioux; one of the most widely circulated pictures of him, that in the big Stetson, was taken nearby (p. 317).

THE GHOST DANCERS AND THE BATTLE OF WOUNDED KNEE (page 108)

Despite the fact that Indian resistance had been crushed more than ten years before, and the Brule and Oglala reservations in Nebraska abandoned,

> fear that the Indians would once again go on the warpath

was omnipresent throughout the developing state. This fear was heightened when the "ghost dance," a ritualistic worship of Wovoka, prophet of the Great Spirit . . . spread throughout the reservations (OHN, p. 146).

As Mari Sandoz tells it in *Old Jules:*

Ever since the reduction of rations in 1887 there had been trouble at the Pine Ridge Agency. The Messiah craze, spreading from the west, aggravated the situation, bringing the Sioux an illusion of hope. Perhaps the white men could be driven forever from the plains. Then once more the Great Father would send the buffaloes forth from the caves of the south, to spread as a moving black robe over the grasslands northward.

Everywhere there was talk of another Indian war. . . . [Settlers] recalled the annihilation of Custer and advocated troops. The first squaw men and breeds that slipped into Rushville and Gordon asking protection sent the settlers into a panic . . . (p. 128).

The war news manufactured by the correspondents was so convincing that even the county sheriff believed in the danger and distributed rifles among the remoter settlers. . . . By the fifteenth of November, 1890, the town of Rushville, the nearest railroad station to Pine Ridge, was swarming with war correspondents; even Theodore Roosevelt, writing for *Harper's,* was there (p. 130).*

The agent at Pine Ridge, Dr. D. F. Royer, was a political appointee and "utterly inexperienced" (SC, p. 254). On 15 November 1890, he telegraphed from Pine Ridge to the Indian Office at Washington that "Indians are dancing in the snow and are wild and crazy," and that "employees and Government property at this agency have no protection and are at the mercy of these dancers" (SC, pp. 262-263). Then came

that incredible incident, the flight of Agent Royer and his dramatic appearance in the little town of Rushville,

---

* Copyright 1935 by Mari Sandoz. Published by Hastings House.

Nebraska, where he is said to have come roaring down the street in his buckboard with his team at full gallop and white with lather, shouting as he tore past that the Sioux were up and that everyone would be murdered. The army reports refer to this incident briefly; eyewitnesses have given colorful accounts of Royer's swift passage down the main street of Rushville. . . . His Paul Revere ride, if it really took place, must have been on November 18 (SC, pp. 264-265).

On 19 November troops began to arrive, beginning with the Negroes of the Ninth Cavalry; and within a few days eight troops of the Seventh Cavalry, eight companies of the Second Infantry, and one battery of the Fifth Artillery were at the agency under the command of Brigadier General John R. Brooke (SC, p. 265).

Buffalo soldiers, as the Indians called the curly-haired colored troops, swaggered through the little town [Rushville]. Impatient to shed blood and emboldened by the potent frontier whiskey, they declared a little war among themselves, whacking a few dark heads with revolvers and smashing a few mouths. After a week of this, the citizens began to wonder if they didn't prefer the Indians, even ghost-dancing Indians. . . .

December first the citizens of Rushville and vicinity called a meeting. . . . What had the Sioux done to justify troops on their reservation? But business men saw that an Indian war meant freighting, a good market for local produce. A Rushville miller contracted 68,000 pounds of flour for the troops. . . .

By the middle of December the excitement among the settlers had quieted down. Not an Indian seen, not a warwhoop heard, and the thermometer hovered about twenty below zero.

Then came the news of the shocking annihilation of Big Foot's band at Wounded Knee; men, women, and children mowed down by Hotchkiss guns while they and their sick chief were surrendering the pitifully inadequate arms and asking for the peace they had not broken (OJ, pp. 130-131).

The killing of Big Foot's band occurred on 29 December 1890, and it was on this night, the author recalls, that people in Rushville were expecting the Indians "to attack the Holy Rosary Mission . . . with the object of taking their children from the school" (see p. 108).

The country between the agency and Wounded Knee was swarming with mounted parties of enraged Sioux who were ready to attack any group of whites they might meet.

Slowly the endless night wore on. No one tried to sleep. . . . As day came, smoke was seen billowing up to the north of the agency, and it was reported that the ghost dancers had fired the Roman Catholic mission. . . . [Colonel George A. Forsyth] found that the mission was not under attack; but a large force of Sioux . . . had set fire to the empty log cabins of the White Bird (Spleen Band) camp. A government day school also was going up in smoke (SC, p. 306).

Early in the New Year, General William A. Miles arrived and took personal charge. An important chief, Young-Man-Afraid-of-His-Horse, "vigorously espoused the cause of peace" as did Chief American Horse. Other important chiefs—Red Cloud, his son Jack, Two Strike, Crow Dog, Little Wound, Big Road—

had been swept away in the panic flight from the agency camp when the first news of Wounded Knee was brought in. These chiefs had been compelled to accompany the mass of frenzied Sioux; but they had now quieted down and were working to separate their people from the ghost dancers. . . . These Sioux from the agency camps were already missing the regular issues of beef and other rations. They were hungry and cold, and most of them were not interested in fighting the troops (SC, p. 308).

By mid-January, the last of the ghost dancers had surrendered.

Photographs confirm the account given by the author's

Indian friend (see page 145) of the manner in which the Indian dead were buried after the wanton massacre at Wounded Knee Creek.

THE HOME GUARDS (page 110)

(The following account was written by the late B. J. PETERSEN *of Rushville.)*

The "Indian Scare," as it was called, brought many interesting events in 1890 and 1891. The writer, with the rest of his family, was at that time living in the east railroad section house, and many a night the house was packed full of families from the country who came there for safety, as they supposed.

Each of the towns of Gordon, Rushville, and Hay Springs had organized a company of militia who were furnished arms and ammunition by the government. A captain among their number was chosen and they would get out every day for a little drill and target practice. WILLIAM ALEXANDER was the captain of the company at Rushville.

However, the real military organization anywhere in this entire territory was known as the "Mosser Guards." Their drill ground was at the Mosser schoolhouse (Milan School), named after one of the early settlers, Philip Mosser. The Rushville *Standard* of March 20, 1891, has this to say about this unique military organization which was composed entirely of countrymen:

This Company of 50 men was organized November 21, 1890 and fully officered with Captain, 1st and 2nd Lieutenant, 5 Sergeants and 8 Corporals; just 6 days afterward, they were armed with the latest model of U.S. Springfield rifles with drop-leaf and globe sights and the "Rice" upper band. The next day they met for their first drill and have had regular weekly drills ever since, without a skip or miss, in spite of storms, blizzards, snowdrifts and last but not least—the Indian scare that paralized for a short season all this upper country. While the surrounding settlers skedaddled to the towns along the railroad for safety, the members of this company remained under their own vine and fig trees, except they usually in squads of 5 or 6 families met in rendezvous at night, fully prepared to furnish Messrs. Oglala and Brule the warmest kind of entertainment.

They are drilling under the Upton system of military tactics, the same as used in the regular army, and as a portion of their officers were also officers of varied and practical experience during the late Civil War, it isn't so very strange that this company should "got there" with "both Feet" as crack amature soldiers, even in the short time they have been drilling. One incidental feature of their drill is a new and novel one; occasionally, each member of this company is required one at a time, to step out of his place in the ranks, assume the bearing, attitude and position of the commanding officer, give half a dozen commands which are executed by the balance until each one has officiated as an officer. This company will never need to "hang their harp on the willows" because some of their officers are away on a visit; neither do they wait for an officer when they arrive at their drill room but as soon as a few arrive drilling commences.

Though the members are strictly agricultural in their avocations, yet at their last drill meeting they declared their intention to adjourn from their plows, harrows and cultivators, and keep up regular drills all summer. In view of the fact that about all the leading educational institutions have companies of Cadets who are drilled in the manual of arms and military evolutions, as a necessary adjunct to a finished education, it seems strange that so few of the localities that called upon the state for arms and ammunition, should neglect to organize the regular military companies and perfect themselves in military science.

Old Man Cunningham (page 105)

" 'Old Man Cunningham' was a veterinarian, according to Mr. Herman Hagel, who is our best authority on early-day Rushville history" (Letter from Mrs. E. A. Winston, Librarian, Sheridan County Historical Society). The author recalls that "Old Man Cunningham and his wife were fat and friendly, but I do not recall Mr. Cunningham doing any sort of work—presume he drew a pension as he would be about the right age for a Civil War veteran. I saw them only as I walked by on the way to town or as I went about my chores with Grant's horses."

Sol Pitcher (page 128)

"Solomon V. Pitcher was the first surveyor of Sheridan County. Pitcher was with the government outfits prior to his settlement at Rushville. He assisted in the surveys in the southwest part of Scotts Bluff county, and was with the party that found the big cedar with a seven foot trunk. This cedar was so near to a proper corner for a section, that it was so designated. Some years later the timber scavengers cut it, but the perpetrators of the deed were never found. A tree seven feet in diameter should make a large number of posts, and no doubt did so, and perhaps kept a homesteader's family from dire hunger" (HWN, p. 426). Sol Pitcher figures prominently in *Old Jules.*

Judge Cornelius Patterson (page 128)

The first county judge, he was re-elected three times

(1885-1891), and served as county attorney from 1903 to 1906.

Judge W. H. Westover (page 128)

"The dean of Sheridan County bar is Judge W. H. Westover. He was pioneer attorney at Gordon, the first county attorney, and has been district judge now these past more than twenty-five years" (HWN, p. 429). In all, Judge Westover served as district judge for thirty years, from 1896 to 1926.

Sheriff Essex (page 132)

W. H. Essex, the third county sheriff, was elected in 1894 and re-elected two years later. He had been preceded in the office by E. J. Rosecrans, whose brother taught at Fairview School during the time the author attended there, and by John Riggs. One of the two deputy sheriffs appointed by Riggs was Nebraska's most eminent cattle rustler and horse thief, David C. "Doc" Middleton. Riggs was a foreman at Hunter's ranch and his brother-in-law, T. B. Irwin, a county commissioner, was foreman at Newman's ranch. "These two were the old and the big ranches of the time. Looking back across the intervening years, it appears that the appointment [of Middleton] was a wise bit of strategy. Doc might not have complete respect for the ownership of horses and cattle, but while deputy sheriff it is safe to say that the stock of Hunter's ranch and Newman's ranch were absolutely immune from the frequent and almost epidemic tendencies of other people's stock to mysteriously disappear" (HWN, p. 426).

Johnnie Jones (page 132)

J. H. Jones was first manager and then owner of the Phinney & Williams lumberyard (HWN, p. 421), and cashier of the First National Bank from 1894 to 1896. He was a life-long friend of Jules Sandoz, and there are numerous references to him in *Old Jules*.

Jules Sandoz (page 132)

Jules Ami Sandoz was born in Neuchatel, Switzerland in 1857. He came to western Nebraska in 1884, "bringing with him his dream of building communities which would have political and economic freedom. He located colonists on homesteads in the Niobrara country, inducing them to immigrate and settle there with his descriptions of how the virgin land could be developed. In 1930 the College of Agriculture of the University of Nebraska conferred upon him posthumous membership in its Hall of Achievement for his pioneer horticulturist work" (*Hostiles and Friendlies: Selected Short Writings of Mari Sandoz*, Lincoln: University of Nebraska Press, 1959, p. 2). *Old Jules*, a biography by his daughter Mari, won the Atlantic nonfiction award in 1935, and made him an American legend. The Modisett ranch (see page 86) adjoined Old Jules' last homestead about fifteen miles farther into the sandhills.

Miss Patience Tulle (page 134)

Prior to teaching at Rushville, Miss Tulle taught the first term at Clinton's first school, in the fall of 1885 (WW, p. 1040).

Mrs. W. W. Wood (page 134)

"The first white child born in Rushville was Wilma Wood, daughter of Mr. and Mrs. W. W. Wood. Mr. Wood was an attorney residing on a claim in the Rush Valley settlement, and later served as Receiver in the United States land office at Alliance. He early moved to Rushville after the advent of the railroad, waiting only to make a final proof on his claim. The daughter was born soon after they moved into the town" (HWN, p. 421).

Ort Sawyer (page 135)

Orson Sawyer was one of the early county agents of the Extension Division of the University of Nebraska. He served in this capacity in Sheridan County for two and a half years, beginning in 1918.

HEYOKA (page 156)

In *Black Elk Speaks* by John G. Neihardt (New York: William Morrow and Company, 1932), the *heyokas* are described as "sacred fools, doing everything wrong and backwards to make the people laugh" (p. 191).

. . . I will say something about heyokas and the heyoka ceremony, which seems to be very foolish, but is not so.

Only those who have had visions of the thunder beings of the west can act as heyokas. They have sacred power and they share some of this with all the people, but they do it through funny actions. When a vision comes from the thunder beings of the west, it comes with terror like a thunder storm; but when the storm of vision has passed, the world is greener and happier; for wherever the truth of vision comes upon the world, it is like a rain. The world, you see, is happier after the terror of the storm.

[221]

But in the heyoka ceremony, everything is backwards, and it is planned that the people shall be made to feel jolly and happy first, so that it may be easier for the power to come to them. You have noticed that the truth comes into this world with two faces. One is sad with suffering, and the other laughs; but it is the same face, laughing or weeping. When people are already in despair, maybe the laughing face is better for them; and when they feel too good and are too sure of being safe, maybe the weeping face is better for them to see. And so I think that is what the heyoka ceremony is for (pp. 192-193).

The following description of the ceremony occurs in *Crazy Horse: The Strange Man of the Oglalas* by Mari Sandoz (New York: Alfred A. Knopf, Inc., 1942):

The *heyokas*, the thunder dreamers, made their ceremonials too. . . . They made the old, old ceremonials before the people, doing everything backwards and mixed up, as they must—wearing their clothes wrong side out or turned around, all singing together instead of one at a time, shivering in the heat of the sun, crawling through mudholes instead of jumping them, pointing their arrows at themselves and falling like dead when they missed, taking meat from the boiling kettles with their hands.

All these things brought much laughing to the people, made them feel new and strong . . . (pp. 210-211).*

See also "The Sun Dance and Other Ceremonials of the Oglala Division of the Teton Sioux" by J. R. Walker, *Anthropological Papers of the American Museum of Natural History*, Vol. XVI, Part II (New York, 1917).

---

* Copyright 1942 by Mari Sandoz. Published by Hastings House.

ACKNOWLEDGMENTS

The University of Nebraska Press wishes to express its thanks to Mrs. E. A. Winston, Librarian, Sheridan County Historical Society, Inc., Rushville, Nebraska, for calling this manuscript to its attention and for her subsequent indefatigable assistance in identifying persons, locales, and dates of events mentioned by the author.

The Press is grateful to Mari Sandoz for unusually valuable aid and counsel during the editing of the manuscript; to Miss Kathryn Duerfeldt and Miss Belle Farman, former residents of Sheridan County, for reading the book in manuscript and checking many details; to Dr. John F. Davidson, Associate Professor of Botany, University of Nebraska, for assistance in identifying Sandhills flora referred to by the author; and to Dr. Donald Danker, Archivist, Nebraska State Historical Society, for checking homestead and timber-claim filings of the O'Kieffe family.

The author joins with the Press in thanking the above-mentioned persons and others on the staffs of the Sheridan County Historical Society, the Nebraska State Historical Society, and the University of Nebraska who assisted in verifying details of his manuscript and in identifying persons, places, and dates. However, the responsibility for any errors or discrepancies is solely his own.

Finally, we wish to thank the following for permission to use copyrighted material: Mari Sandoz and Hastings House for permission to quote from *Old Jules* and *Crazy Horse;* John G. Neihardt and William Morrow and Company for permission to quote from *Black Elk Speaks;* George E. Hyde and the University of Oklahoma Press for permission to quote from *A Sioux Chronicle.*

[223]

THE PIONEER HERITAGE SERIES

In the volumes of the Pioneer Heritage Series, the University of Nebraska Press proposes to present the Trans-Missouri West of frontier days, not as it appeared to the movers and shakers, the doers of mighty or evil deeds, but seen through the eyes of the people history happened to—the families and individuals whose "grand strategy" was simply to survive. It is our hope that their stories—preserved in diaries, letters, journals, interviews, and recollections such as this one—will enable the reader to perceive the American frontier experience with a new immediacy, with a solid awareness of how it felt to be living on these plains a hundred, or seventy-five, or fifty years ago. For this reason, no less than for their intrinsic interest and their value as social history, the University of Nebraska Press believes that the books of the Pioneer Heritage Series comprise a distinguished and necessary contribution to the literature of the Great Plains. Volume I of the Series is MOLLIE: THE JOURNAL OF MOLLIE DORSEY SANFORD IN NEBRASKA AND COLORADO TERRITORIES 1857-1866.